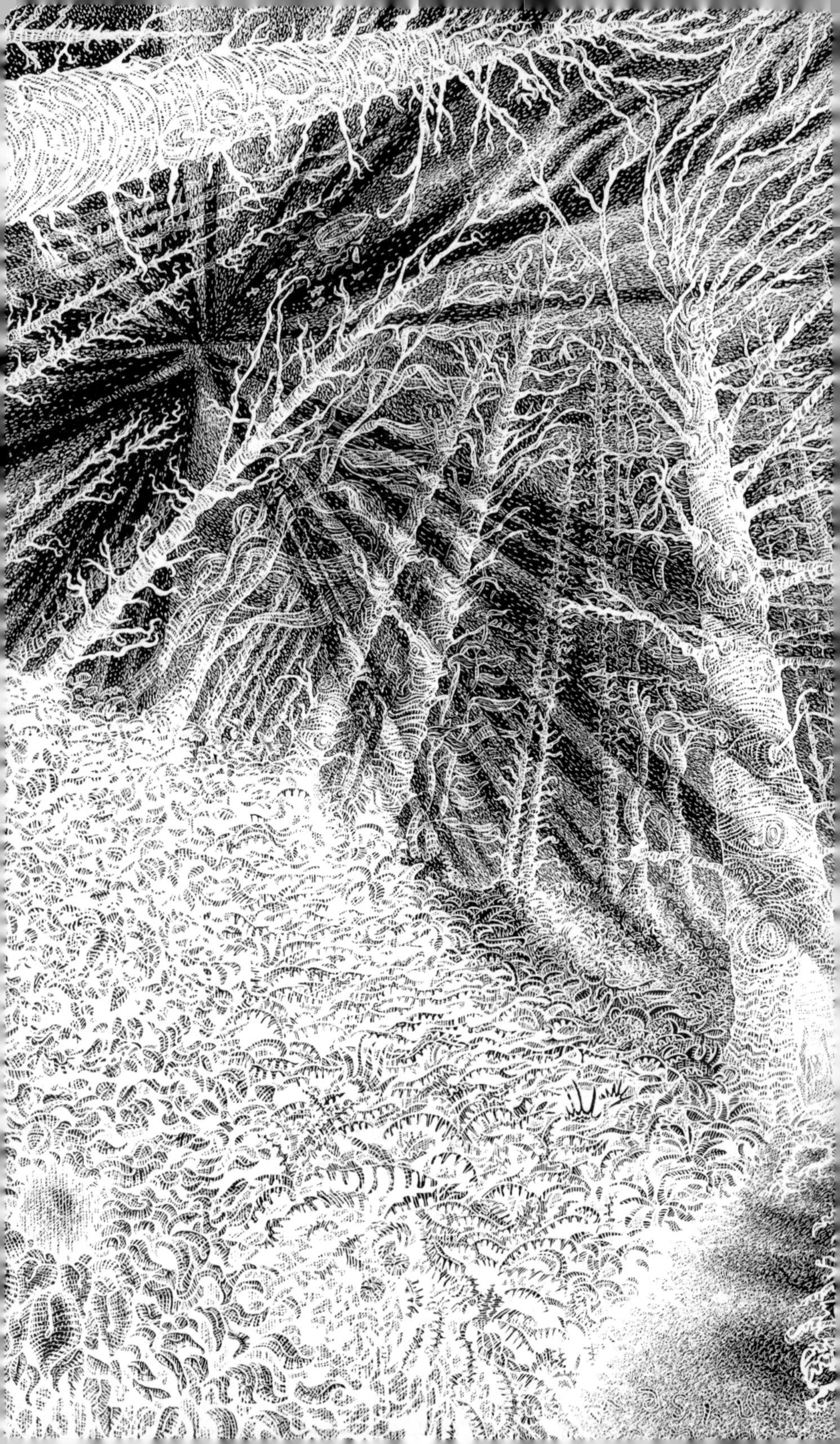

PINEAL FORESTS

ALSO BY MICHAEL H. KEW

Crossings
Rainbownesia
Nectars of Sky
Purplēdeneye
Incense Gardens
Swahilia

PINEAL
FORESTS

Wheel of Life on the Southern Oregon Coast

Michael H. Kew

SPRUCE
COAST
PRESS

Copyright © 2024 by Michael H. Kew

All rights reserved.

Spruce Coast Press
Chetco Range, Oregon

michaelkew.com
@michael.kew

U.S. Library of Congress Cataloging-in-Publication Data
LCCN 2024902180 | ISBN 9798989402915 (hardcover)
Author, American—21st century | Oregon, Pacific Northwest, Nature, Spirituality, Metaphysics, Ecology
LOC record available at http://lccn.loc.gov/2024902180

Cover: "Oregonghost" by Spencer Reynolds

Unless noted, all photographs by the author
Artwork by Spencer Reynolds   *artandsurf.com*
Cover design by Sarah Reed
Interior typesetting by Jess LaGreca, Mayfly book design

Manufactured in the United States of America
First Edition

CONTENTS

map	viii
preface	ix
Bird-Here-Now: *January*	1
Pineal Forests: *February*	21
Skyhalation: *March*	37
Flower Phoenix: *April*	53
Kins of May: *May*	71
The Time We Carry: *June*	83
The 15%: *July*	95
Blue Moonity: *August*	111
Crimson Quest: *September*	121
October in the Haloed Earth: *October*	135
Trinity Topaz: *November*	147
Undead in the Evergreen: *December*	157
about Curry County	173

For Tank and Mini Marvin

T. 30 S.
T. 31 S.
T. 32 S.
T. 33 S.
T. 34 S.
T. 35 S.
T. 36 S.
T. 37 S.
T. 38 S.
39 S.
40 S.
41 S.
19 N.
P
A
C
I
F
I
C
Langlois
Denmark
Blacklock Rock
Tower Rock
Castle Rock
Gull Rock
Cape Blanco
The Heads
Rocky Pt.
Redfish Rocks
Coal Pt.
Island Rock
Sisters Rocks
GEISEL MON. STATE PARK
Needle Rk
Pyramid Rk
WEDDERBURN
GOLD BEACH
BUENA VISTA STATE PARK
SEBASTIAN STATE PARK
Cape Sebastian
Hunters I.
HARRIS BEACH STATE PARK
Crook Pt.
Mack Reef
Natural Bridge
Whale Head
House Rock
Cape Ferrelo
Goat Island
BROOKINGS
Chetco Cove
COOS
CURRY
Bancroft
Remote
Kenyon Mtn
UMPQUA NAT'L FOREST
Hood Mtn
Powers
Bingham
Iron Mtn
Panther Mtn
Brushy Mtn
Lobster Hill
Kimball Hill
Skookumhouse Bu
Wildhorse Prairie
Lawson Bu
Saddle Mtn
Sugarloaf Mtn
Grizzly Mtn
Snow Camp Mtn
Windy Valley
Mineral Hill
Quail Prairie Mtn
Lately Prairie
Red Rock
Pollywog
Vulcan
Red Mtn
Chetco Pk
Mt. Emily
Standard
Gold Basin
Josephine Mtn
Parallel
Collier Bu
Red Flat
JOSEPHINE
CURRY
CO
ROGUE
RIVER
R. 3 W.
R. 1 W.
R. 10 W.
R. 1 E.
R. 3 E.
R. 4 E.
9th
OREGON
CALIFORNIA
CURRY
DEL NORTE
CO

PREFACE

What's your year?

Maybe it's another chunk of school—an anniversary—a big fill-in-the-blank holiday—another ritualistic weave of planning, plowing, planting, harvesting—always more sunburn and fever of cabin.

Perhaps it's a lenticular spell of box-checks—tax file, insurance premium, auto reg, membership and subscription due, union due, interest, credit card fee, 12 mortgage or rent, property tax, medicinal copay.

Perhaps it's a scintilla of baseline millennia—calendars lunar, solar, lunisolar. All future anthropologies and archaeologies of you and me.

The ancients would link cyclix with star trails for the first known traits of timekeep. Moon as metronome. Lunar vibes were absorbed later into the Islamic and Jewish year. Later still the Egyptians adopted solar, rooting their new 12-month almanac in the pre-dawn rise of Sirius (Greek: "glowing"), then and now the brightest of eye stars.

In the West (specifically Italy), Romulus's 10-month chronology was circa 45 BCE lengthened by Caesar whose version was circa 1582 CE revised by Pope Gregory XIII whose version is now Earth's permanent civil calendar.

Oh, the corrugations. Always two equinox, two solstice. Recurring cyclix of light and dark—the holy calligraphy of seasons. Numerology, theology, astrology, mythology. Noise and the eloquent ring of silence. Life's ordinary and extraordinary. The churn and seethe of crises, conflicts, blisses. Sickness and wellnesses. Rites of passage. Births, deaths, starts, and stops.

So—what's my year?

In your hands lies '23 loosely. Twelve beads strewn upon a heavily soaked rope—wet with rainfall, snowmelt, sap. Dripping with tears. With river water, ocean water, springwater. With coffee, nectar, booze, and sweat.

Orford Reef. Photo: Jill Elliott

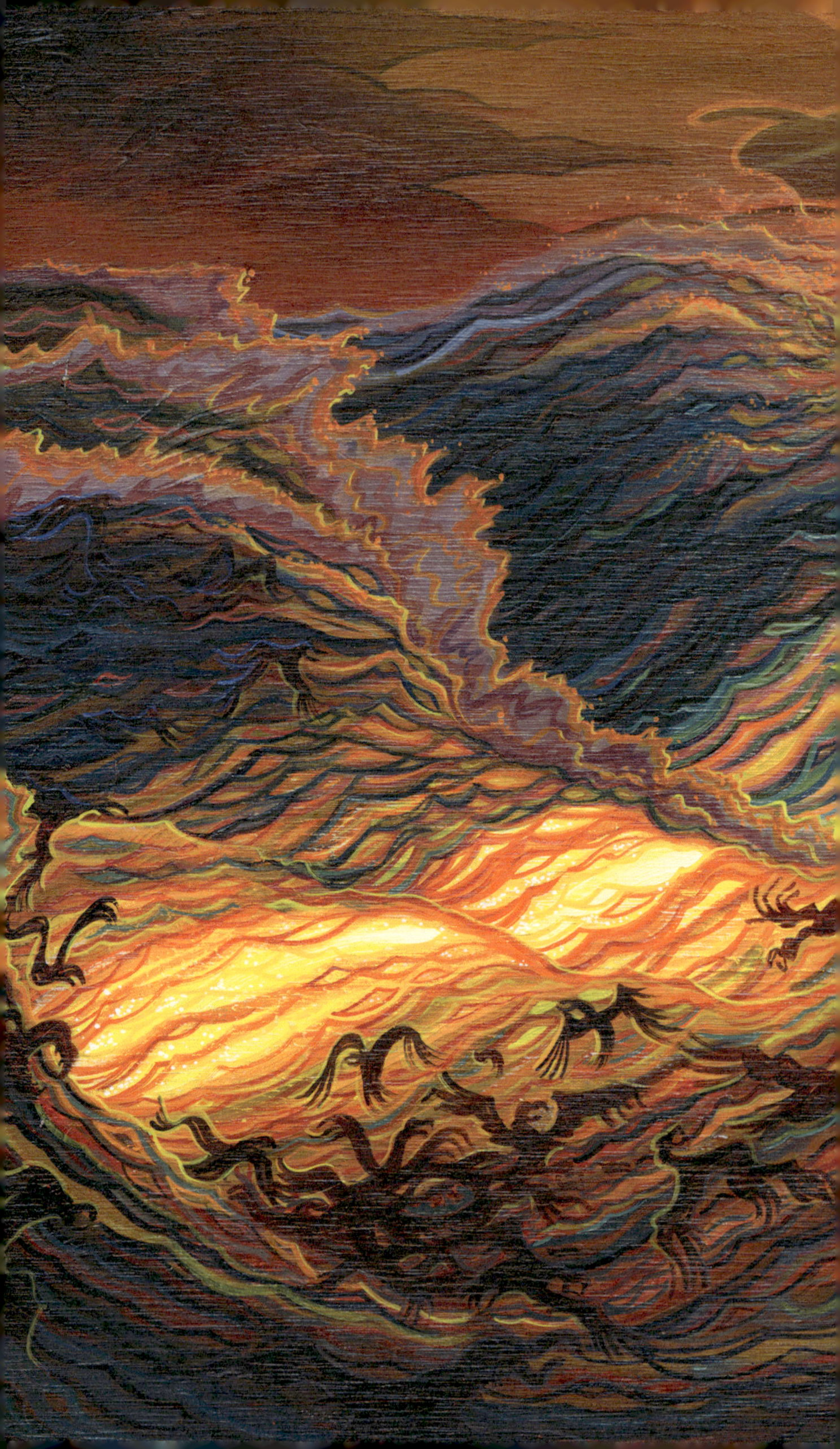

BIRD-HERE-NOW

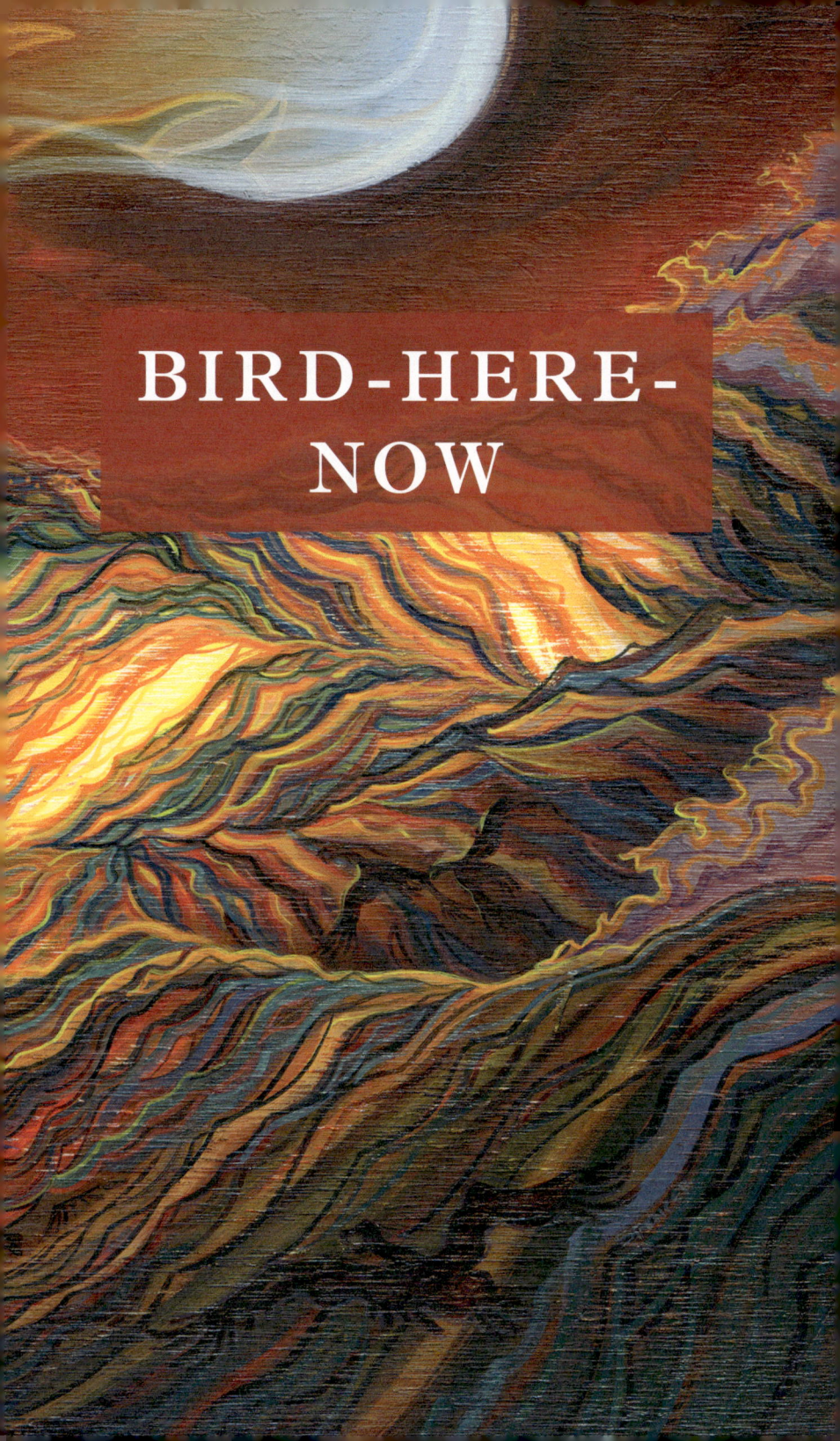

Wee puffs flit from corvidian croaks—wee clouds from louding *wonks*—voluminous dents thrust into the still of dawn chill.
Hunchbacked, he struts and stares.
wonk-wonk!
Between smooth small long-interlude sets, Oregon's ocean is quiet, lakelike—lapping. Slow southeasterly Sun is levitating, backscratching the tall black serration of Sitka spruce pressed against winter dry-spell sky against low seaside ridge of rocks and holy ravendom.
[bob-weave-bob-weave]
Relishing the cardio effects of swimming, my breathing braids with his rhythm. Breathm. Rapid exhalations relaxing to renewed reality of being on land.
wonk!-wonk!-gurgle-gurgle
A riddle?
Raven smarts, yes. Abstract of mind. "Bird-brained" is not an insult.
Facing the wave and skirting the cove's high-tide line lies a thin white film of frozen brine debossed with talon tracks in loops of inquiry. Back and forth he steps and cross-steps, scruffy neck feathers fluffed, long hooked beak ejecting micro-exhalations of CO_2. Rejecting and accepting nothing.
gurglegurglewonk!wonk!
After I'd dug a rail and fallen, the leashless single-finned surfboard had lazed up onto our shaded gray-sand arc of privation. I'd bodysurfed in and crouched 'tween board and raven's ice patch that is destined for mist, for ice breath—beach yet to

eer the early Sun, itself a spiritual inversion of the Cold Moon just now plunging toward horizon behind our rough tufted cape a half-mile north.

[weave-bob-weave-bob]

wonk!

Wee clouds. Visuality of spiritbreath.

I sit and smile at him. Momentum pause. Cross-legged, shift weight to hips, flexing toes inside blood-warmed wombish membrane of bootie juice, fingers in gloved glory, spine straight, gaze fixed out over the surf. Slowly <inhale> a vast cold lungful.

Hold.

Amid this floaty tranquillity I note further descendence of heart—pulsed heat—and raw upper body vaporizations through five millimeters of black neoprene.

Dermal mist. Skin breath.

wonk!

Ravens—North America's biggest songbirds. Fey skysingers of white magic. Feathered black cats. Playful. Manipulative, communicative, decisive, deducive, emotive. Our twinly twined breaths are blown west to mingle 'mongst sea-smoke evaporations—48° water into 30° air. Morning shadows dance upon the murk—shreds of high cirrus and changeling light mooding offshore against the sheer black crags of basalt. Realm of gull and oystercatcher, murre, puffin, cormorant.

Raven skips from crust of ice now tickled clear by sunlight and fattening tide—slithery beach breath, the peak of which will soon spawn sloshy backwash and drown the surf spot in, out, refreshing and energizing, respiring revolving door of moony magnetism.

On the ice's edge, raven's head is reflected. Prompts thought of Janus, Roman god of passageways, looming month of January eponym, infamously two-faced animistic spirit

And my sight eases, soft-focus, blurring to the rhythmic Pacific risings and crashings, the constant cosmic reabsorptions, the winter whites wheezing, water the masseuse of sand and rock, blue veneer a gateway, surfing as ceremony.

Flecks of Sun tap sea-stack tippy-tips of Twin Rocks. My eyes slip shut and scene falls mute into an open plane of silence. Recall some old words by zenmonk mystic Merton: "Prayer? Prayer is how I breathe . . . The gate of heaven is everywhere."

<Exhale>

wonk!

Raven and I—deeply inside.

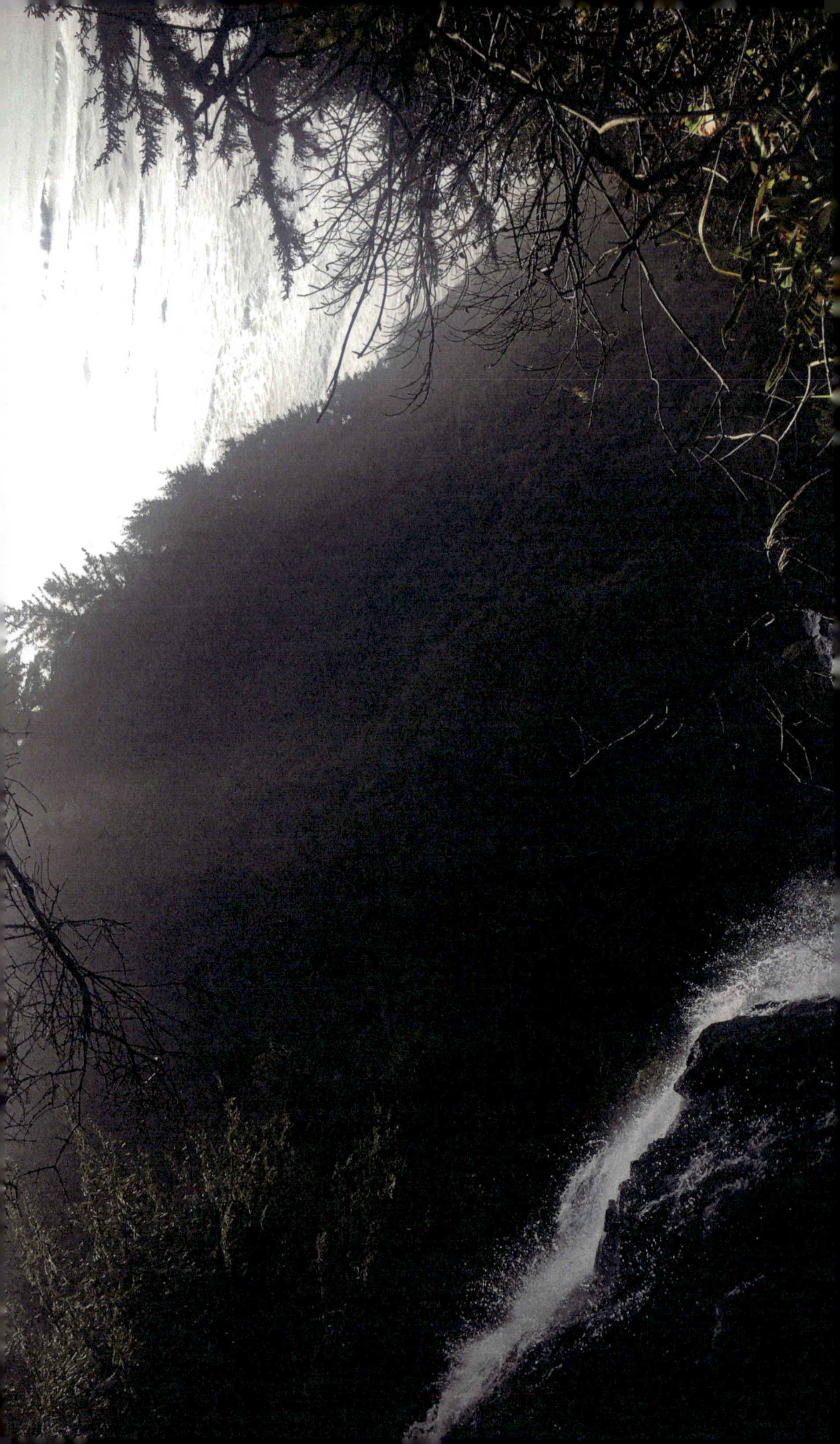

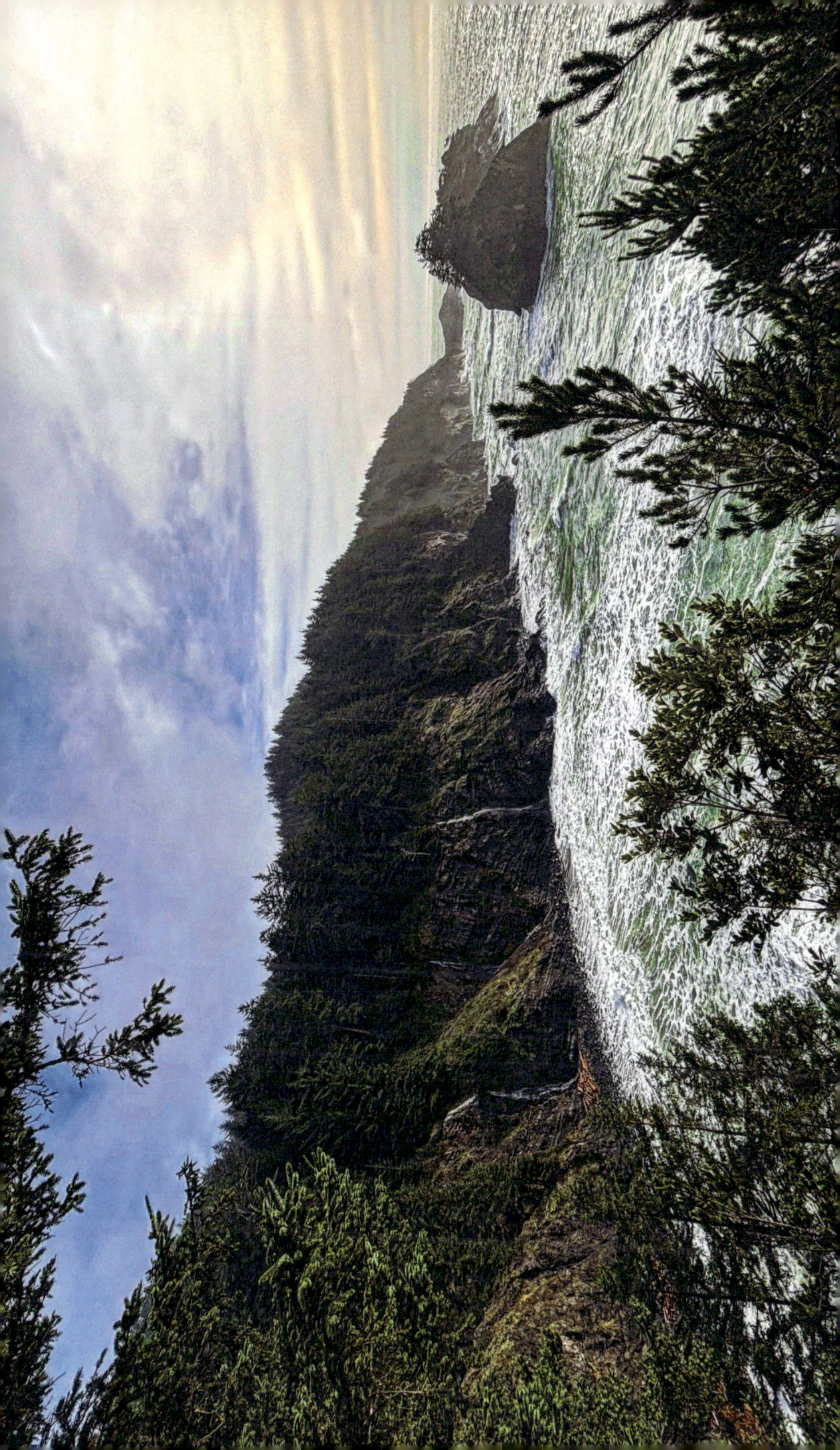

Wolf Moon

Chetco Range

Samuel H. Boardman State Scenic Corridor

Spencer Reynolds

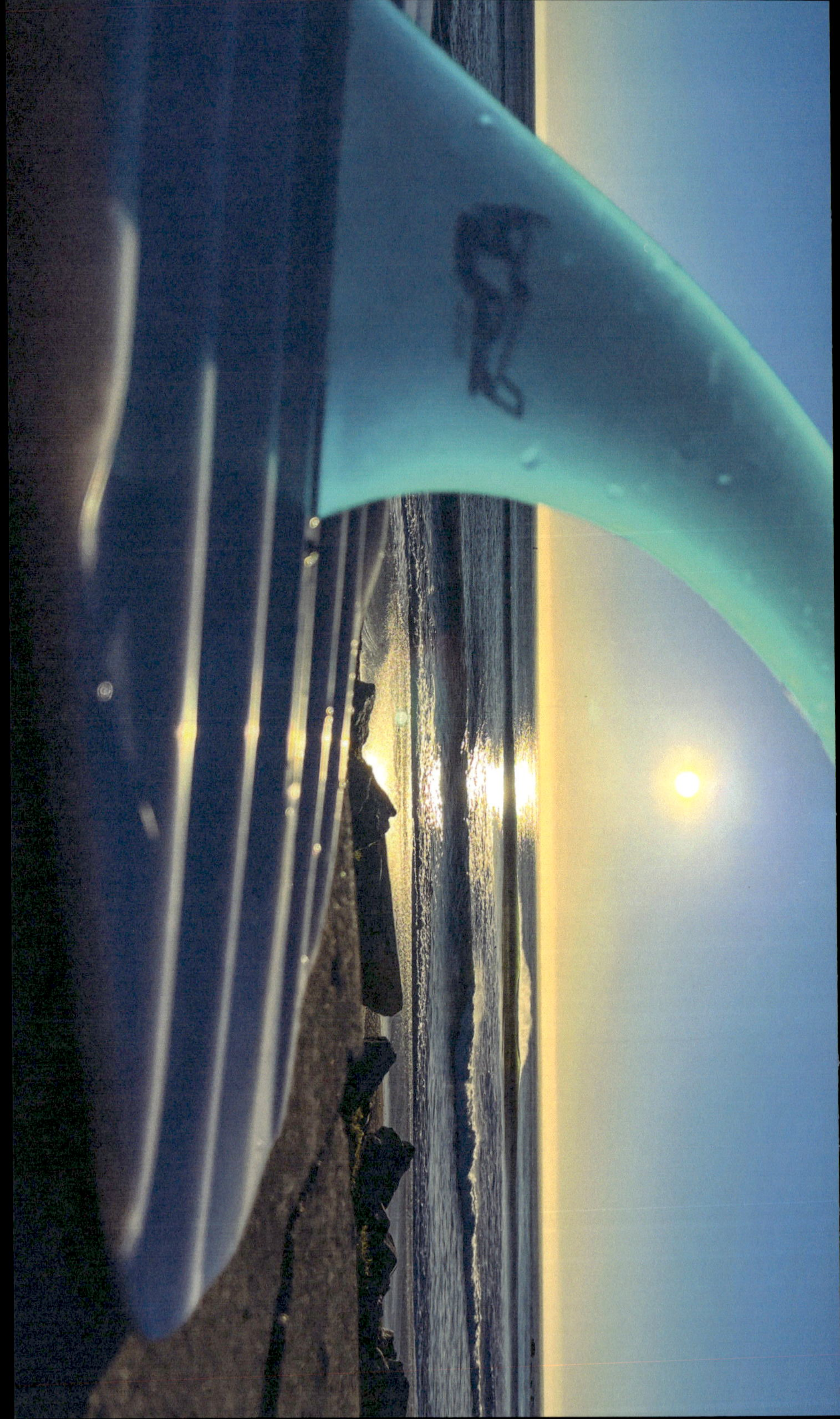

Thirty-foot swell at Indian Sands

Atop Cape Sebastian

Raven

Harris Beach

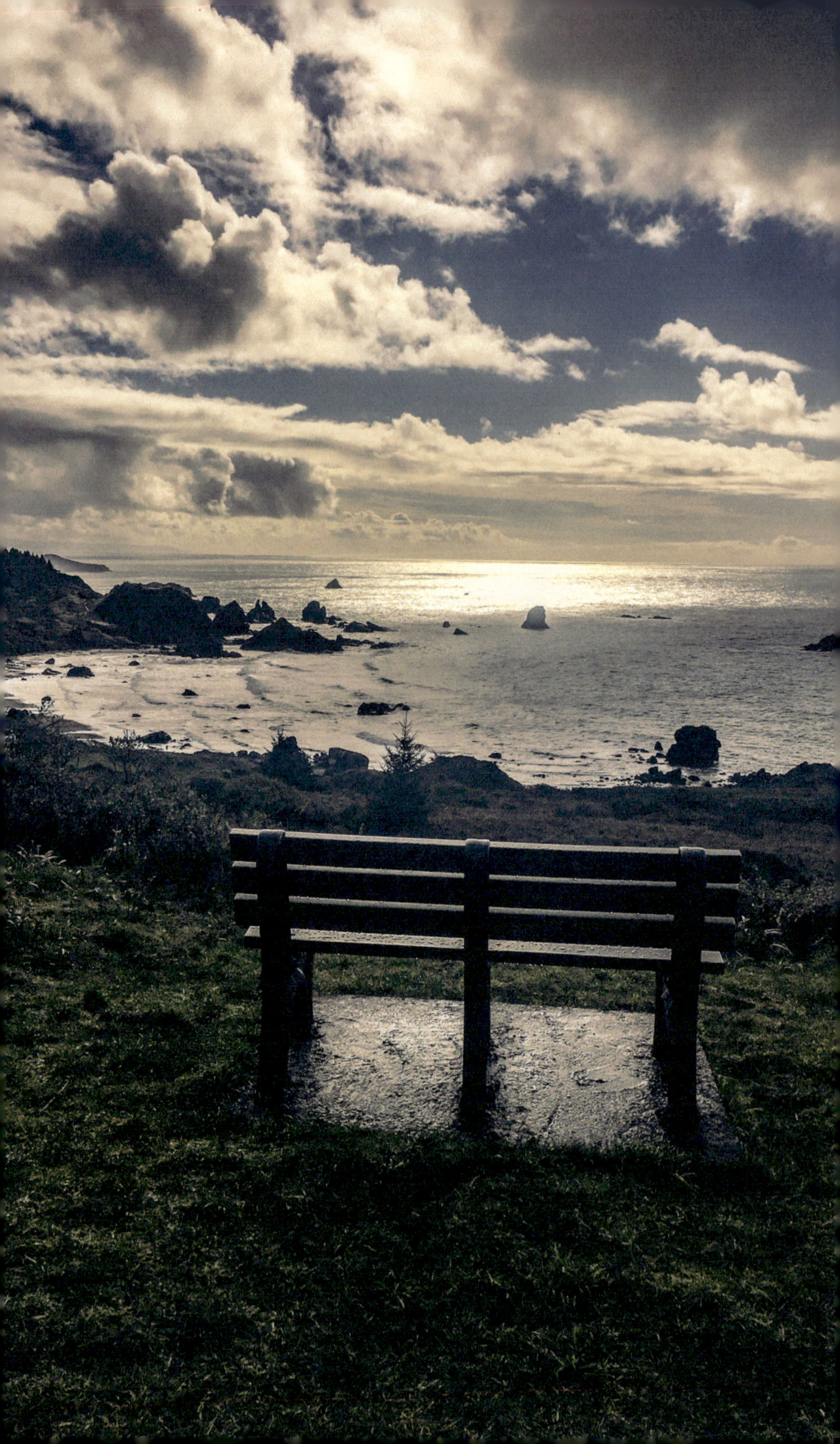

Kalmiopsis

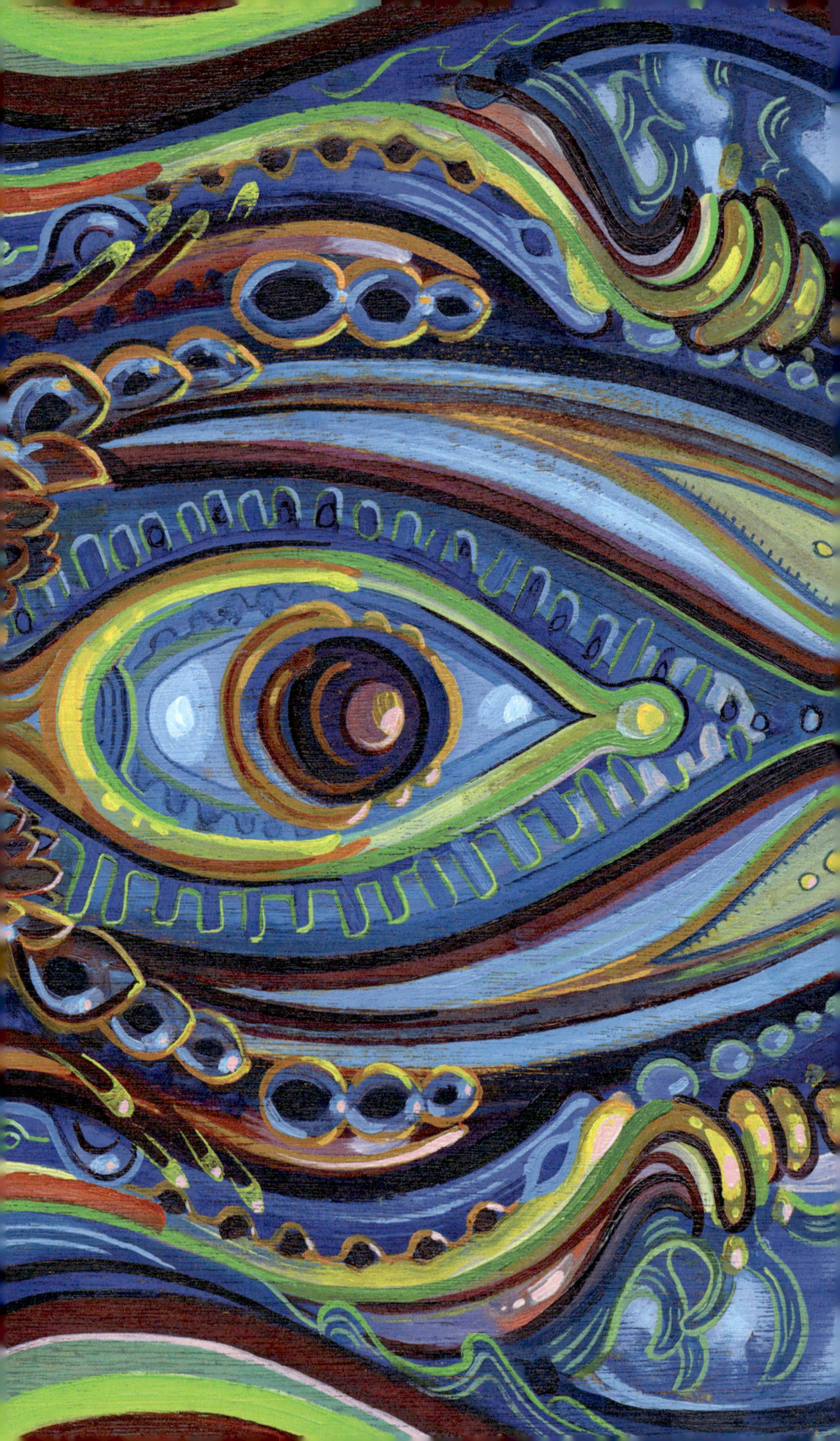

PINEAL FORESTS

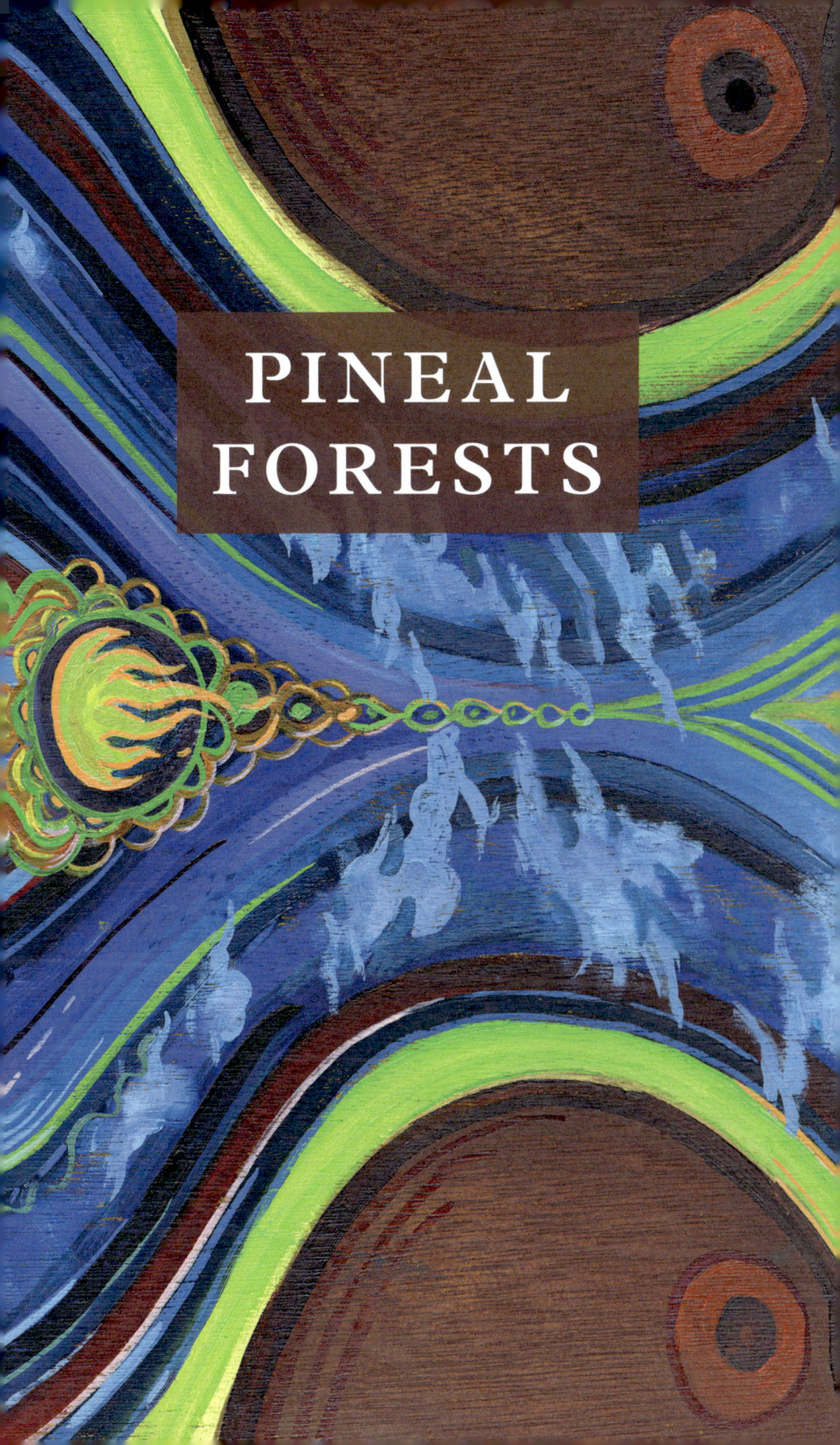

My bed drifts heavy with dreams. Black dreams. With fear and frail fantasy—dooms of death and depression—anxiety and mortal awareness—nostalgic pains in sylvan silence.

But I'm roused by midwinter moonlight, again oiling the exfoliance of nature, my yonic friend. Lubricant for this hole in my brain laced with its ever-brittle threads of a midlife dread.

Rise and step into luxuriance of lunar flower. The pale flood of comfort. Psychonomic zen as a halo wreathes its gibbously-waxing Snow Moon.

Mountain home is the sacred garden. Calligraphies of river and wee-hour whims wheeling past the coastal range, a great sweep of bucolia where upon exiting starry bliss and entering blue-hour revival my mind mires in springwater coffee, knowing all this to be a tender axis mundi of transience and cardinal spin.

South: Rivervalley roll to the beach. Pastel raws of winter. Early obscurities and intimate distances. Long shadows are speared from steep slopes. Green jags and misty drainage folds. Sparkling yellow meadows of dew and deer. Voluminous conifers, gaunt deciduous. Frosty roofs—fir fires flaming up through shaded stovepipes.

Fishermens' silhouettes aside the Chetco's steaming grooves that for 55 miles wend pristine privations to public from 3,700 feet up—through deep wildfire wilderness and the national forest of February, down and 'round my bedroom to be sloshed down and out between rough gray city-limit boulders into the Pacific where my bright memories lay freed from the deeps.

Blink. Sense that? Your pineal gland. Tiny yin-yanging endocrine gem. The pine cone-shaped melatonin-secreting Horus eye inside your third ventricle. Yes, third eye—your valvular circadian eye—and, per Descartes and Shiva et al, the link between realms of physical and spiritual.

Spiritual hours brighten to a day made absolute. My car—a portal. Listen to the latest Roger Eno album. To Yo-Yo Ma versions of *Ave Maria, Thaïs (Méditation), Wiegenlied (Lullaby)*.

Hear that? *Whoosh* of surf reveals a lullaby too.

Beach is befogged. Yet my dense mood untangles to trim time over the ephemeral sandbar. Ocean is amniotic and surfing is pagan baptism: immersion, self-affusion, aspersion by rainbowed spindrift in sunny days, seared here on the sword of northwesterly wind.

Cloudward I squint into the gloom attempting to grok today's (Feb. 2) synchronic global rites of Imbolc, Old Irish Gaelic for "in the belly" (of Mother Earth) and "to cleanse oneself" per adult spiritual rebirth. "Sin" here is subjective. Hopeful minds are purged and atoned. Contemplations of the precise equidistance between these two holy seasonal poles—dark (winter) and light (spring). Our month itself was named for Februa, a purification ritual (on Feb. 15) in the old Rome calendri; *februum* is Latin for "religious purification."

West: Sudden seabreeze clears the sky but wrecks the surf. Sinfully.

East: Return upriver into the new glare and upridge to my distant past. January snows are gone from high red crags of the Kalmiopsis. I ease into the abundant sanctuary of southern Oregon's coastal mountains in winter's lull of "false spring"—another Februic ritual. Its light lifts largely and stirringly, magnifying nature's dormant divinity.

Pineal.

Pine-EE-uhl.

Pine!

North: A gravel prairie road near my property. Elevation 2,000 feet. Strange solstice-equinox musing (and car) serendipitously swerve toward a grove of small flaky-barked pine trees. Here in poor rocky soil amongst the post-Chetco Bar Fire (2017) regrowths of ceanothus, bush chinquapin, and manzanita, I spy personally sacred specimens of *Pinus attenuata*. Knobcones. Their fragrant sticky resin is a salve—antiseptic, antibacterial, anti-inflammatory. Their barbed and serotinous ovoidal cones require fire to crack open and release seed. From dark to light—propagation by the will of flame.

I sit quietly with one of the young pines. Upon a low fractured limb seeps resin. I press a pea-sized dab of it against the center of my seasalted forehead. Lay on dead grass in birdsong with eyes closed as sunlight fills the future amber. Drowse comes quickly—a resinous reverie—and through this I sip the nectar of solar order, sentience soothing and drifting me back into dreams. To vital sweet dreams.

Because in darkness there truly lies light. It just needs to find you.

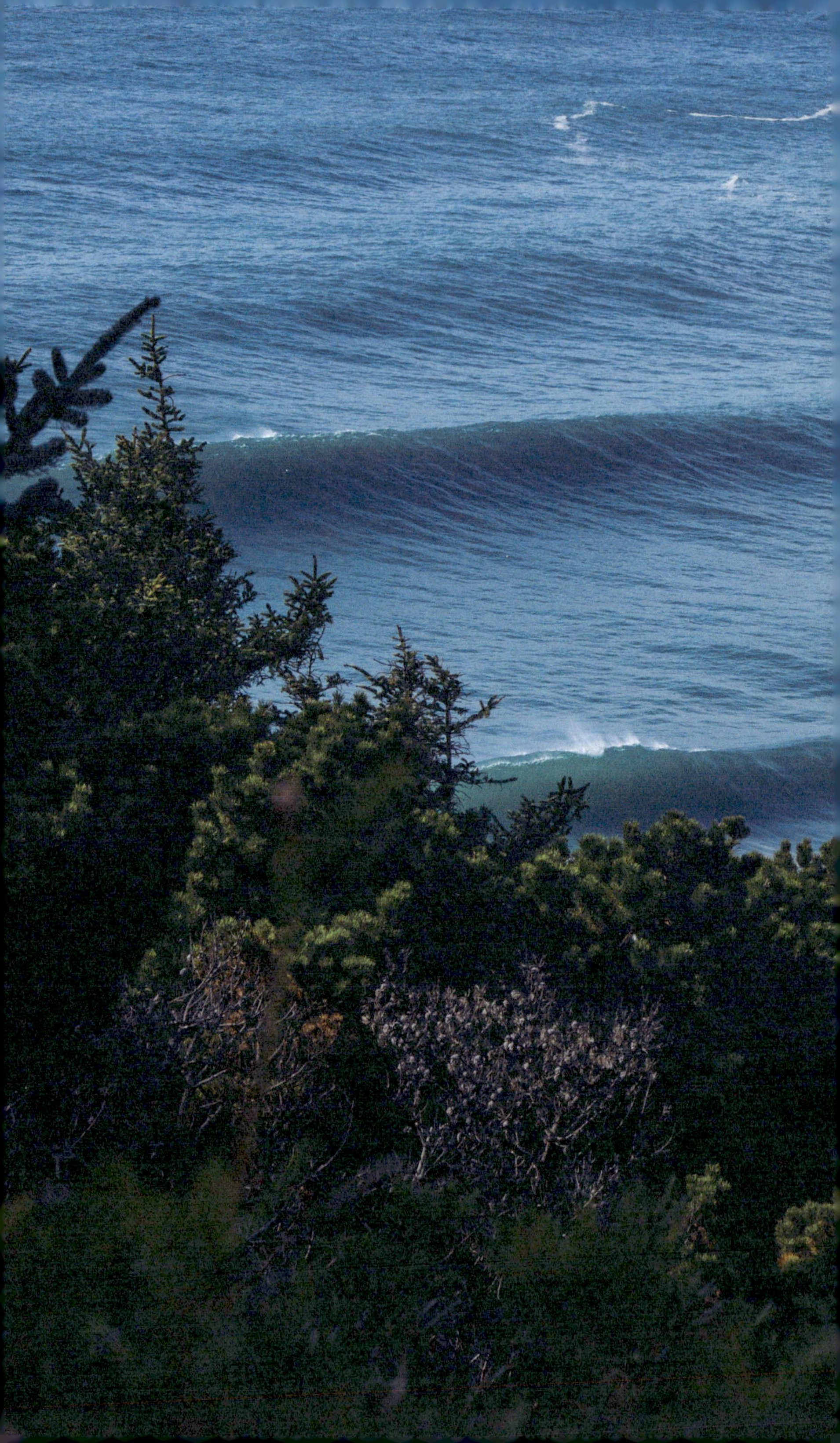

Kalmiopsis rainsmoke

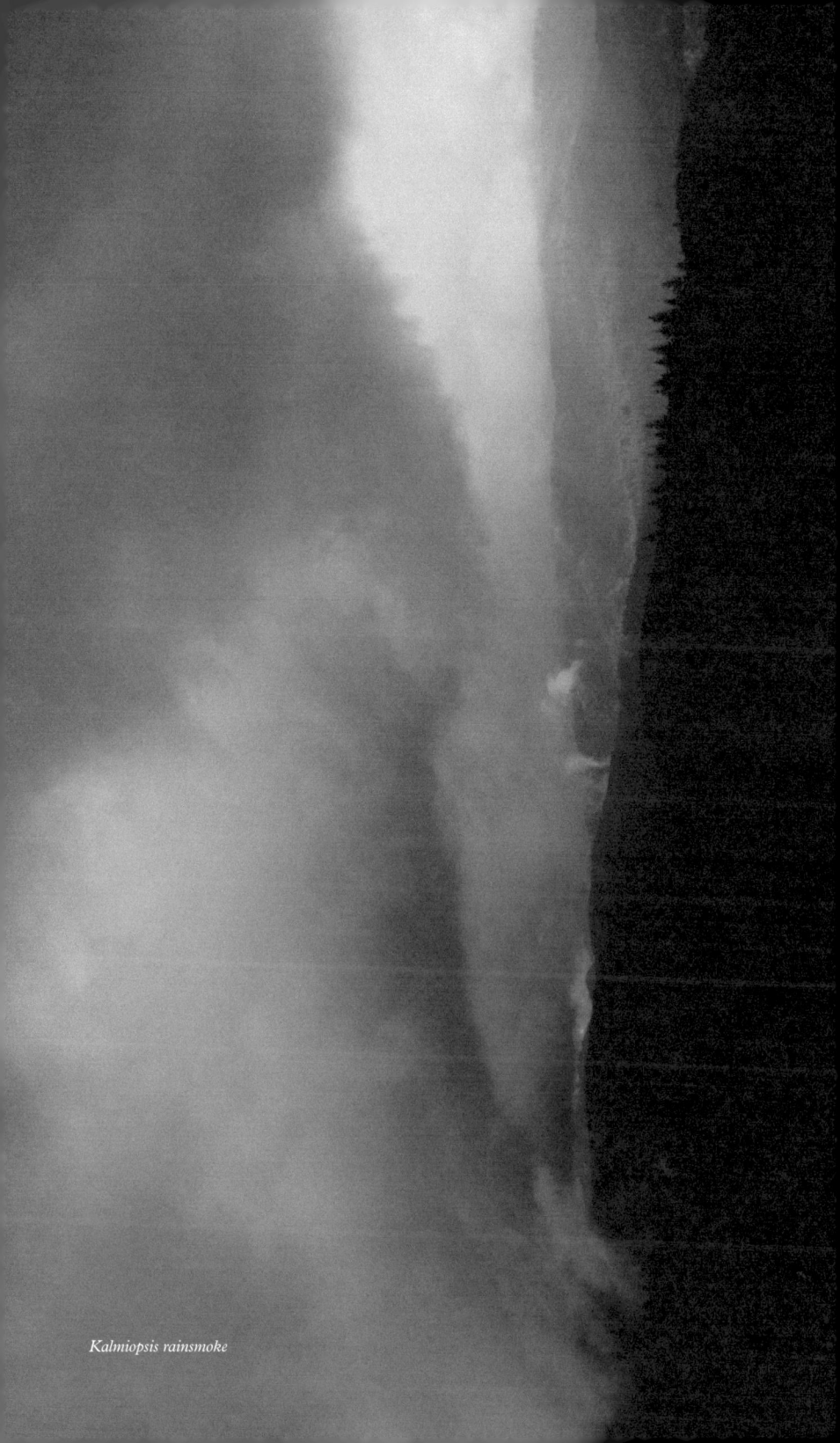

Pistol River

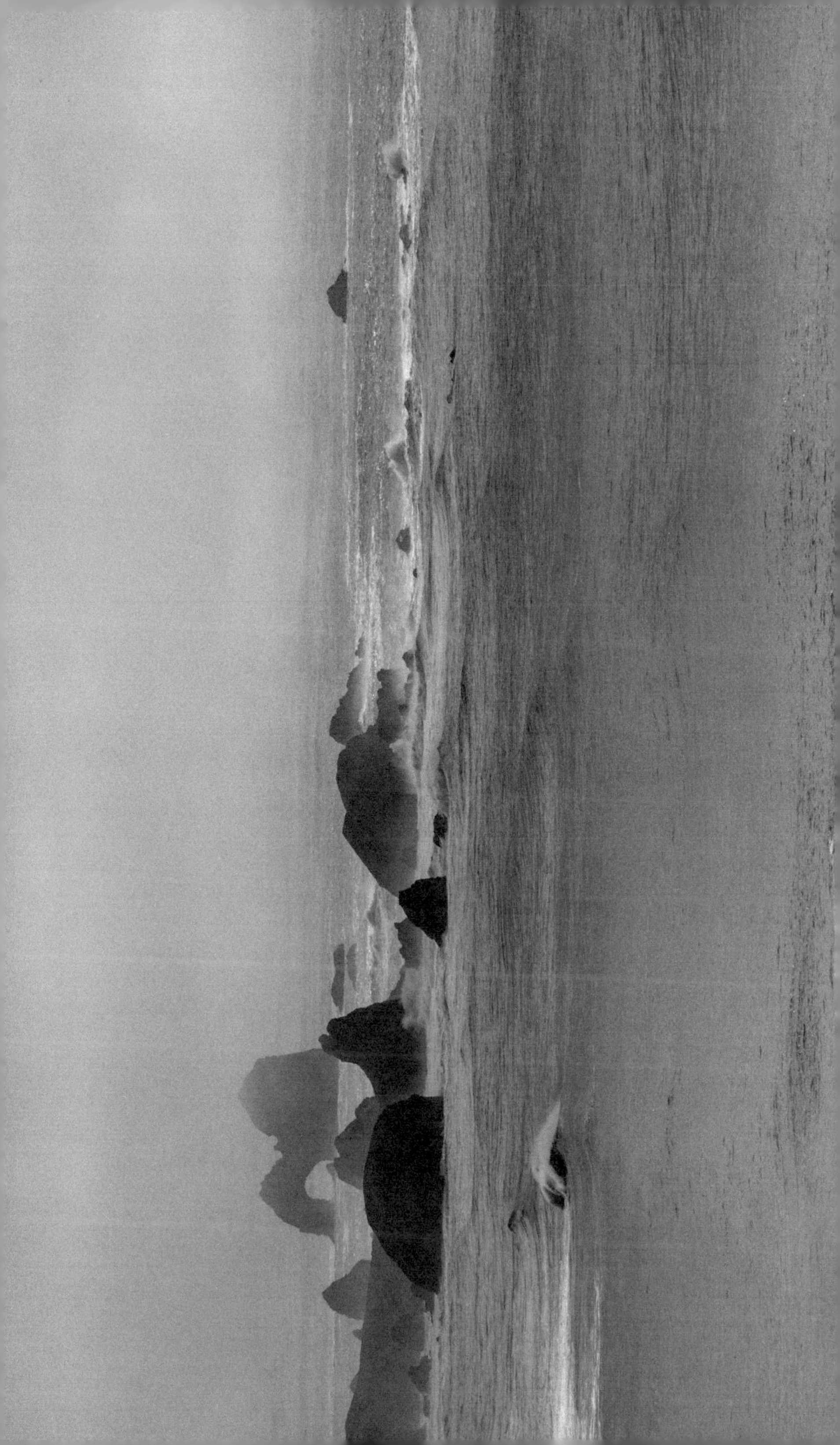

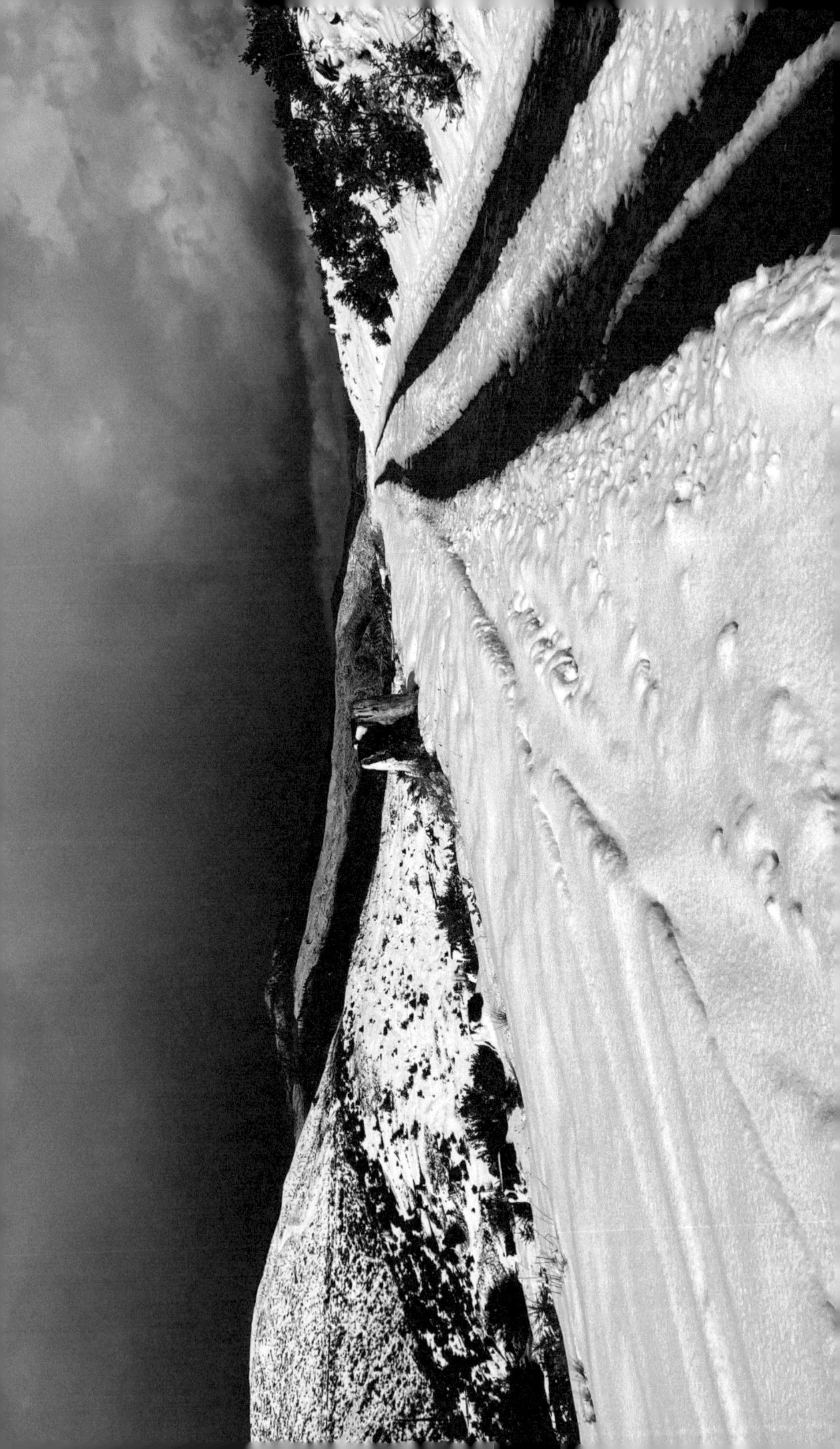

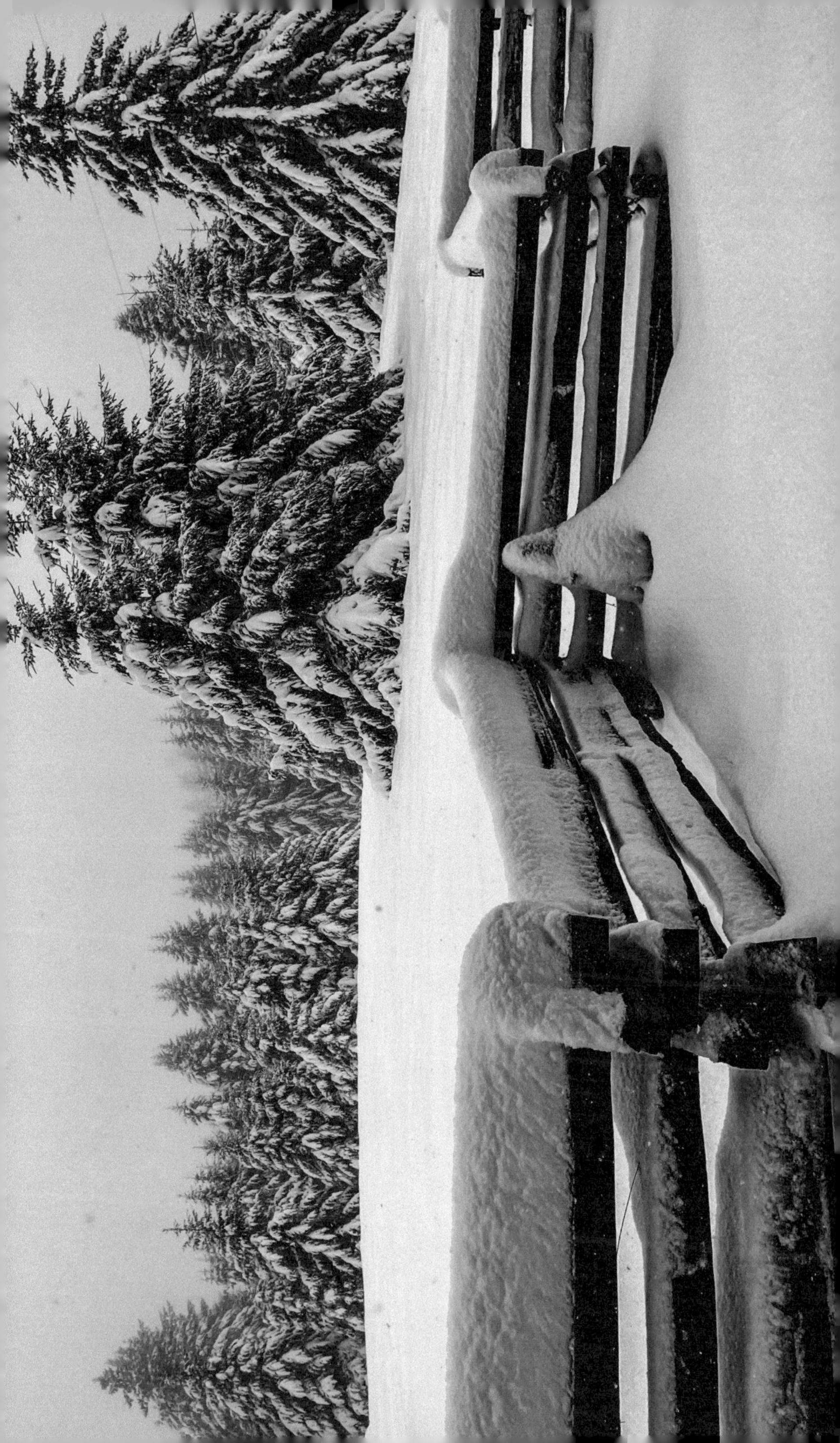

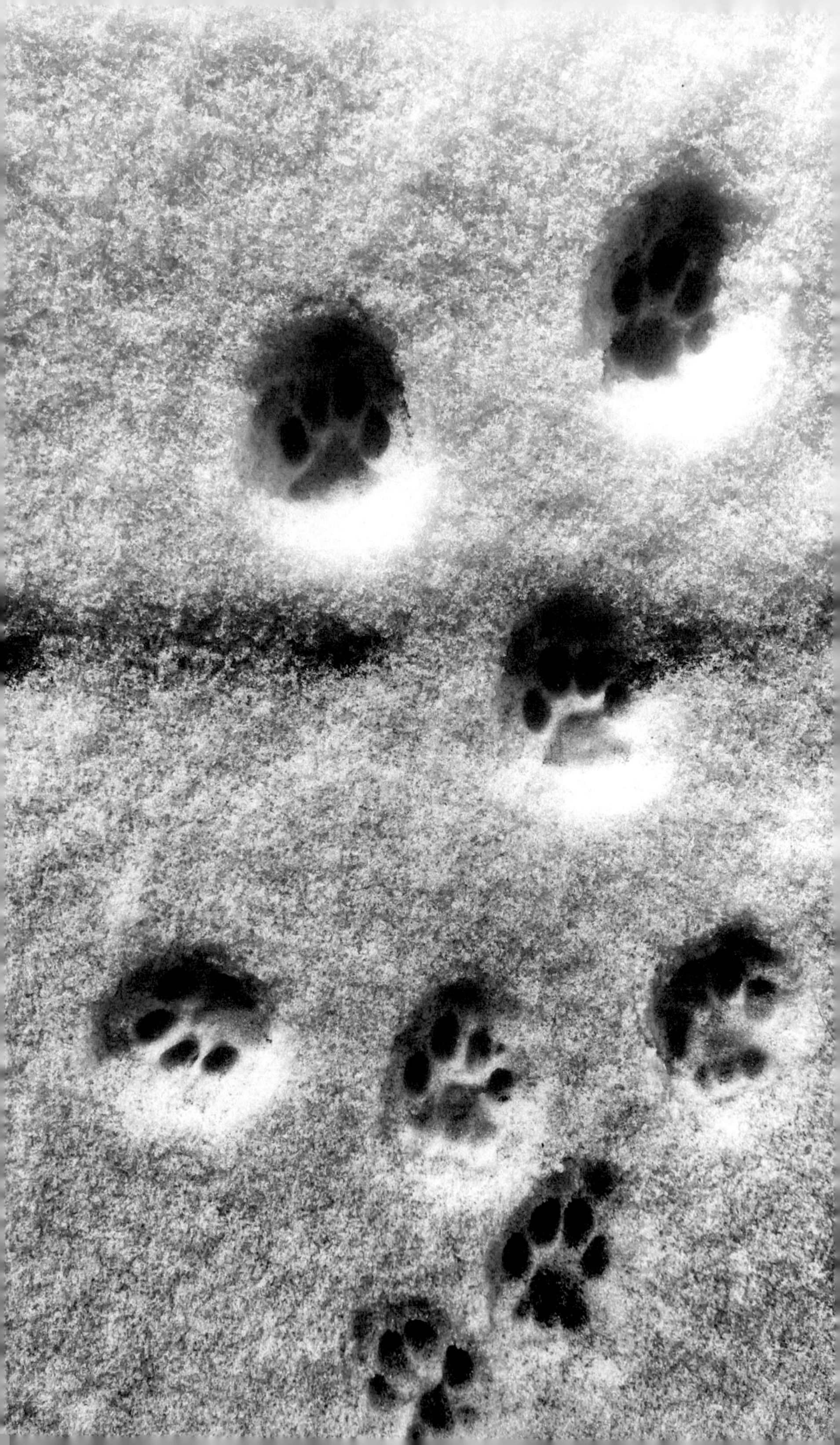

Mount Emily

Knobcone pine

Chetco River

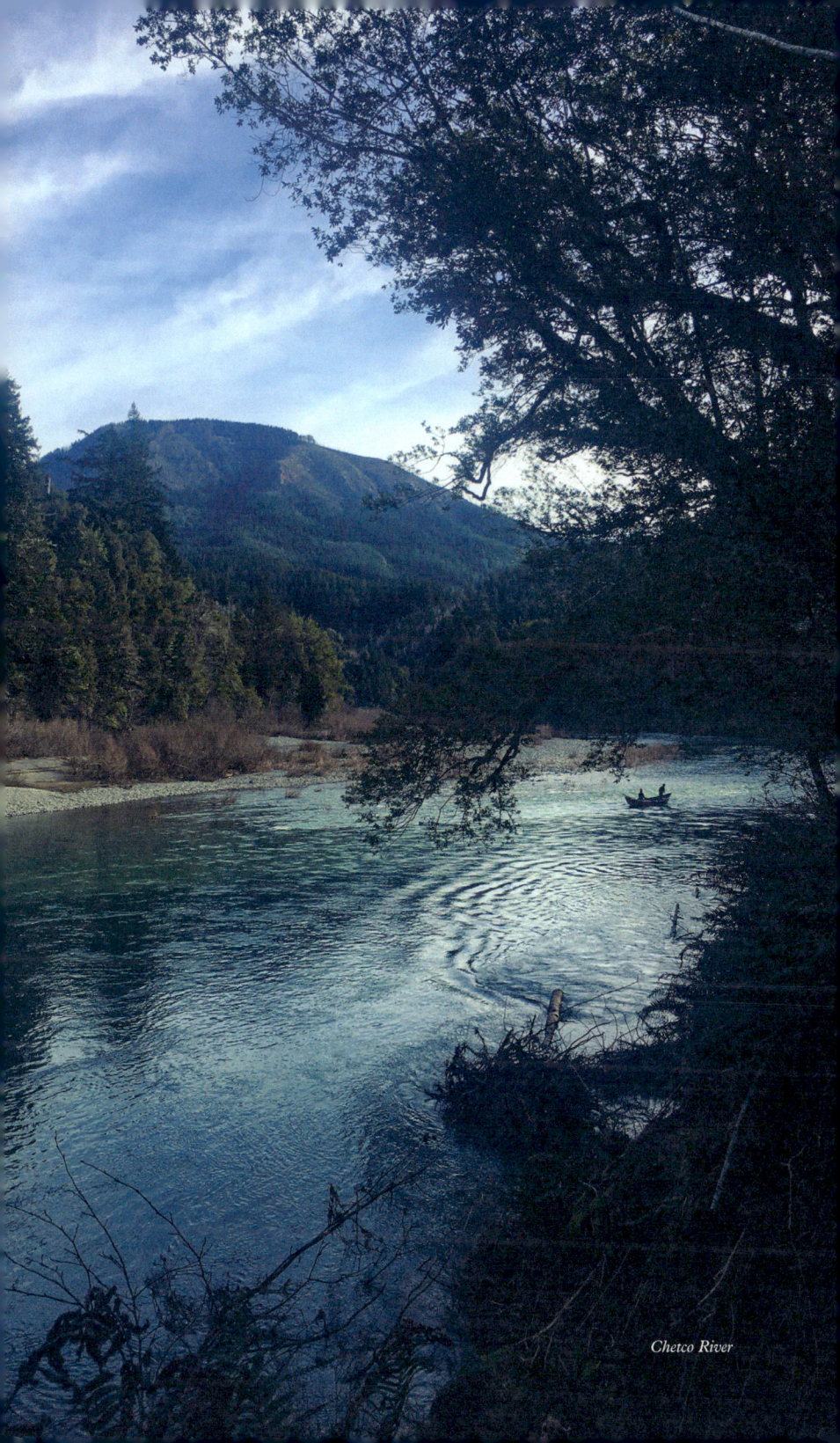

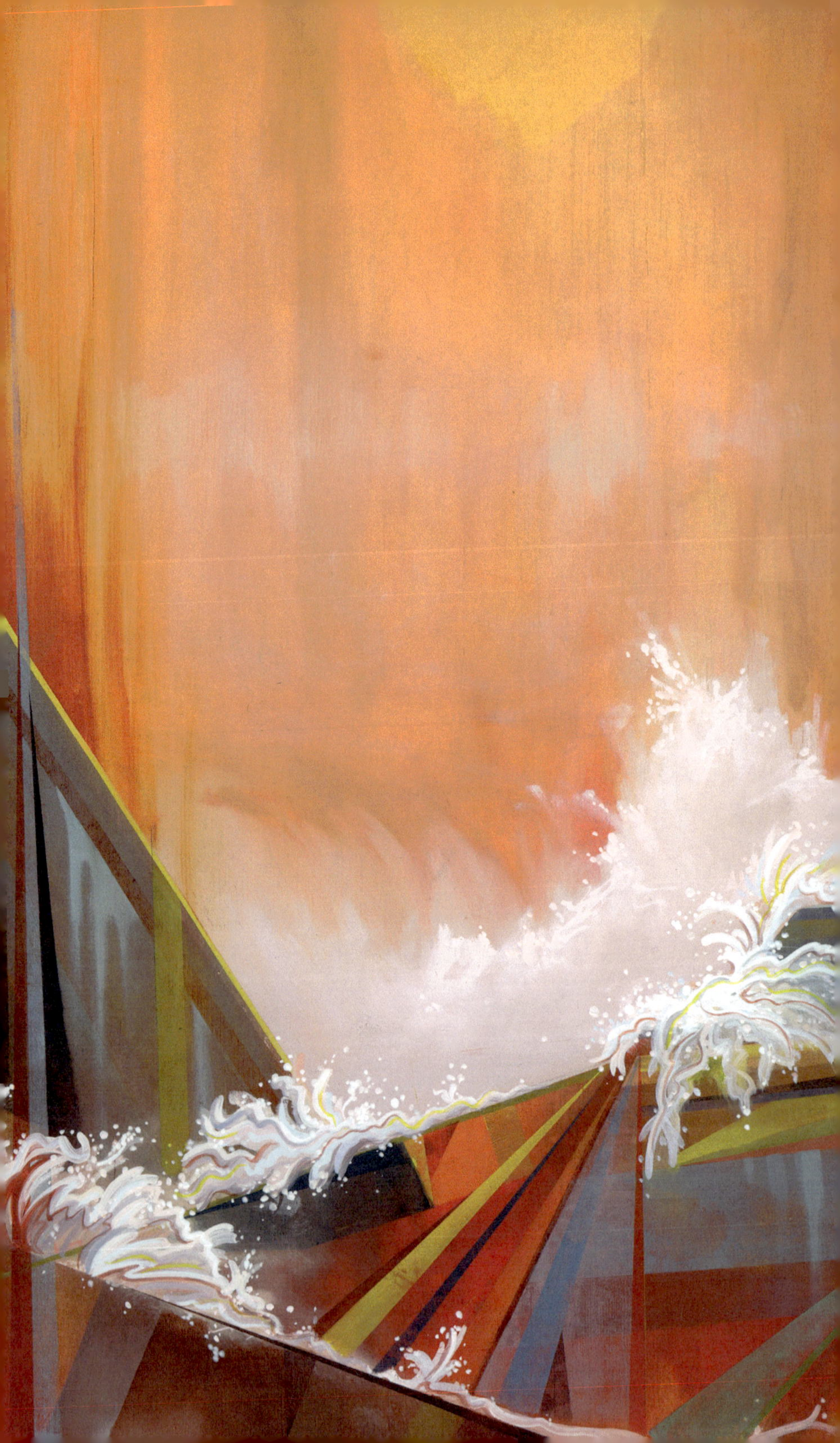

SKYHALATION

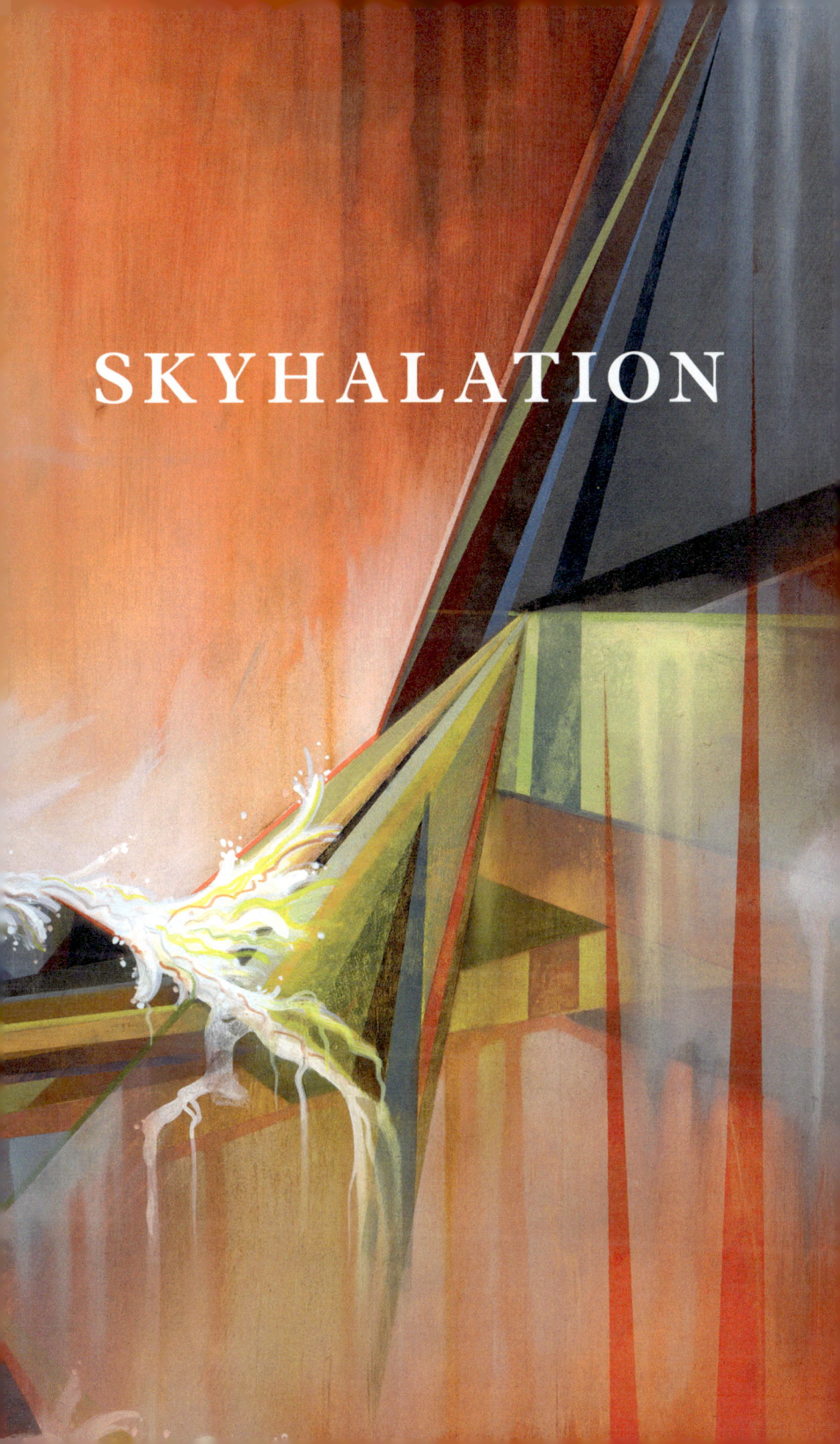

Since Ash Wednesday, a sweet solo doe has found shelter: my back deck, a rough roof of Port Orford cedar. We can see each other through my study's window. Together we lounge and watch the sky exhale—sleet, snow, rain, graupel. Out between storm suites and sleeps she carefully hoofs, poking holes several inches into the drifts. Her grassy browselands are snuffed. And so she strips normally ignored evergreens—rhododendron, toyon, manzanita, even the wavyleaf silktassel near the stairs. Fare of undesirables. All 'round the house and adjacent hills, as the snow keeps falling and falling—desperate leaf depletions. The plants erase to ferny sprouts of black wire begging through frozen crystal. Until they can't.

For the first time, I crave grace from perversions of late winter, from the irrepressible black storm train of Alaskan gulf and its lure of arctic lobes.

This afternoon's snow fleetingly shifts to sleet against skylight and the rash of grayscale against cloud. Gale surges and whips the white off tall conifers, boughs bowing—shuffling—shedding—and by nightfall the sky itself will crack.

Grace!

Squint into the fusion. Portal to cosmic floods. Upon these woods and prairie is a static deep glow unto the ashen echo of spinning constellations. I walk on slippery deck—startle dozing doe—and gaze straight up into Orion's belt. Beneath Gemini Moon the air smells of ice. Out west simmers a long-distance love affair—the first of March's five planetary conjunctions. On the same ecliptic longitude Venus and Jupiter flare, soon subterranean with Earth's axial shift, these two white spider eyes in the pastels presaging equinox, the month by day a growing shine.

Thin pale scroll of cloud sweeps the firmament like an off-season Milky Way. Wheeling panoramas of transcendence slip me into "A Stream With Bright Fish" (Budd/Eno 1984), "stream" here being the astral dance, "fish" the stars.

But heavens will always reseal and weighten. By deep night the mysteries swell. House power again fails.

Heavy snowfall—a sinister silence.

New three-meter fissure above the kitchen table drops a scratch of white gypsum dust onto the brown floor. I drink wine and drowse to purr of woodstove fan. At 1 a.m. I'm shock-waked to more sleeplessness, to more cracks and creaks from manufactured-home roof nearing its structural failure. Don earbuds with the upbeat *Bach With Pluck!* album. Try to relax and ignore imminence.

No.

Pinnacle to decades of incremental snow-load sag. A losing kiss with gravity.

Poppy-creaky-cracks crawl beyond dawn, a watery gray haze, reverb of white and wind whence I can see the night's surprising new 12" upon yesterday's surprise 14 and surprise 15 the night before that, sheeting the prior two-week base of regular but mellow snowfall that was then fun and novel.

Along my ceiling I can also see the new large stress fractures and mutations. Each one pings a pang of paranoia. Chill fills the home. The snow's pressure is sharp knifemetal to the back of my neck.

Power remains out. Road to main road is impassable. The snow continues. Fifty inches here is historic, my elevation just 1,650 feet and six miles from the Pacific.

A rush of nervous phonecalls—area residents, 911, sheriff,

farm tractor quickly clears road and driveway. A miracle. Bless him. Friend with jacks and lumber barely arrives via large 4WD and installs peaces of mind between floor and ceiling. Bless him.

I wonder about Miss Doe—what can she eat now that truly everything is buried?

Plunge down-mountain in first gear through blizzard with my three crying senior cats. Slide out at Dusty Lane. Regroup and reach vacant Brookings house, a refuge gifted by another friend. Bless her.

Sadly the doe and I would miss the Worm Moon, so-named for the rise of earthworms into a hemisphere ostensibly softened by season. In Old Rome, March was the year's first month. Earth would begin warming from winter's grasp into elongated sunlight. Equinox was near—Ostrana in pagan worlds. A brilliant solar festival. Rebirth, fertility, renewal.

I'll need a new roof.

Ensuing three leaden days of snowshoeing in from the county-plowed road to unknown house health. Each time, I expect the worst.

Lonesome slog of roof-clearance. Rakes, shovels, salt pellets. Mounds gather 'round the perimeter. Shards of ceiling crash and others bowl deeper; beams groan upon jacks. The wind shrieks. Snow seethes down and later is only made denser and heavier by sleet thinning to thick drizzle which soaks and pierces my panicking bones.

Day four. Still no doe, no new hoofprints in snow. By midafternoon the atmosphere uncoils, ushering not snow nor sleet but a roar of hard rain across the suffocated land. Galeswept and beaten, slowly the snow sulks forlorn and begins to look neolithic in the misty gray, its tumuli distorting and eroding to hammered platinum before eventually vanishing as vapor.

Vanquished by milder air and the shave of wind, days five and six lay zestfully buoyant. With no new snow, the thawful land flings alive with drip and running water refilling the greeny-brown hues of nude forest. Conifers again shed. Stains of soil and drowned flora reappear. Shrubs and seedlings emerge timidly, thrashed by the wind but again free and abreath.

Melt has never sounded so marvelous.

Day seven dazzles with further promise. Sky flexes into an enormous blue. Midmorning I roll up the mountain upon open roads. A golden interlude to properly shore the home until permanent repairs in coming months. Tomorrow the cats and I return.

And here she is, a tropism, Miss Doe dishing in full Sun on warmed earth edging my eastern yard. Her coat has unmatted. She's a nyctinastic bloom, reopened and beaming beyond the cold. Time has slowed from stormy frenetics.

She stares into me, sunlight irrigating her large globed eyes. Leisured and deliberate, she maws madrone leaves. I imagine us here both pushing praise for the Sun. For grace. And for roofs. By month's end there would be more snow. More freeze. But it would also be spring. She knows today is our turn. Our turn, briefly, to exhale.

photo: Luke Mathison

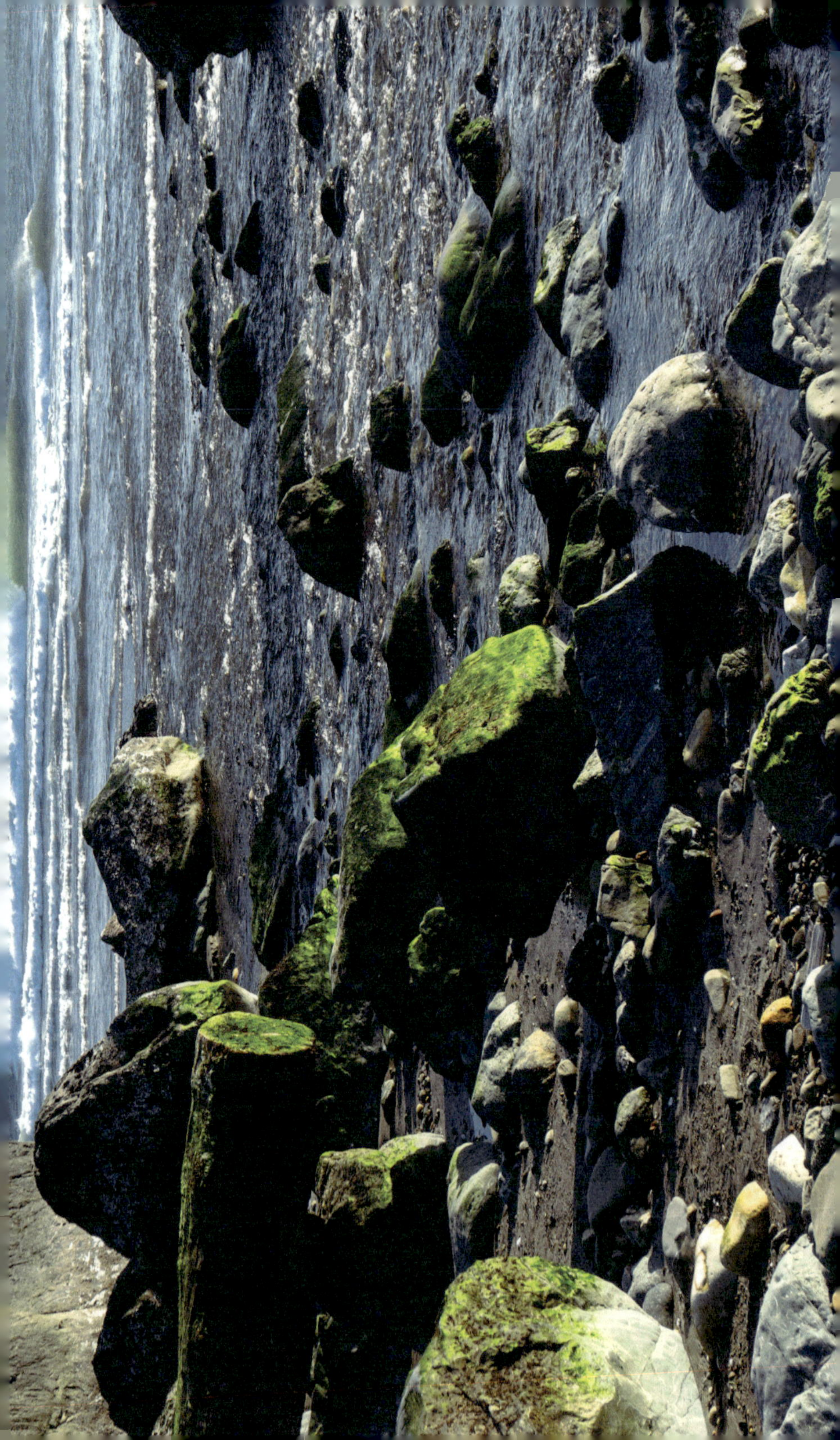

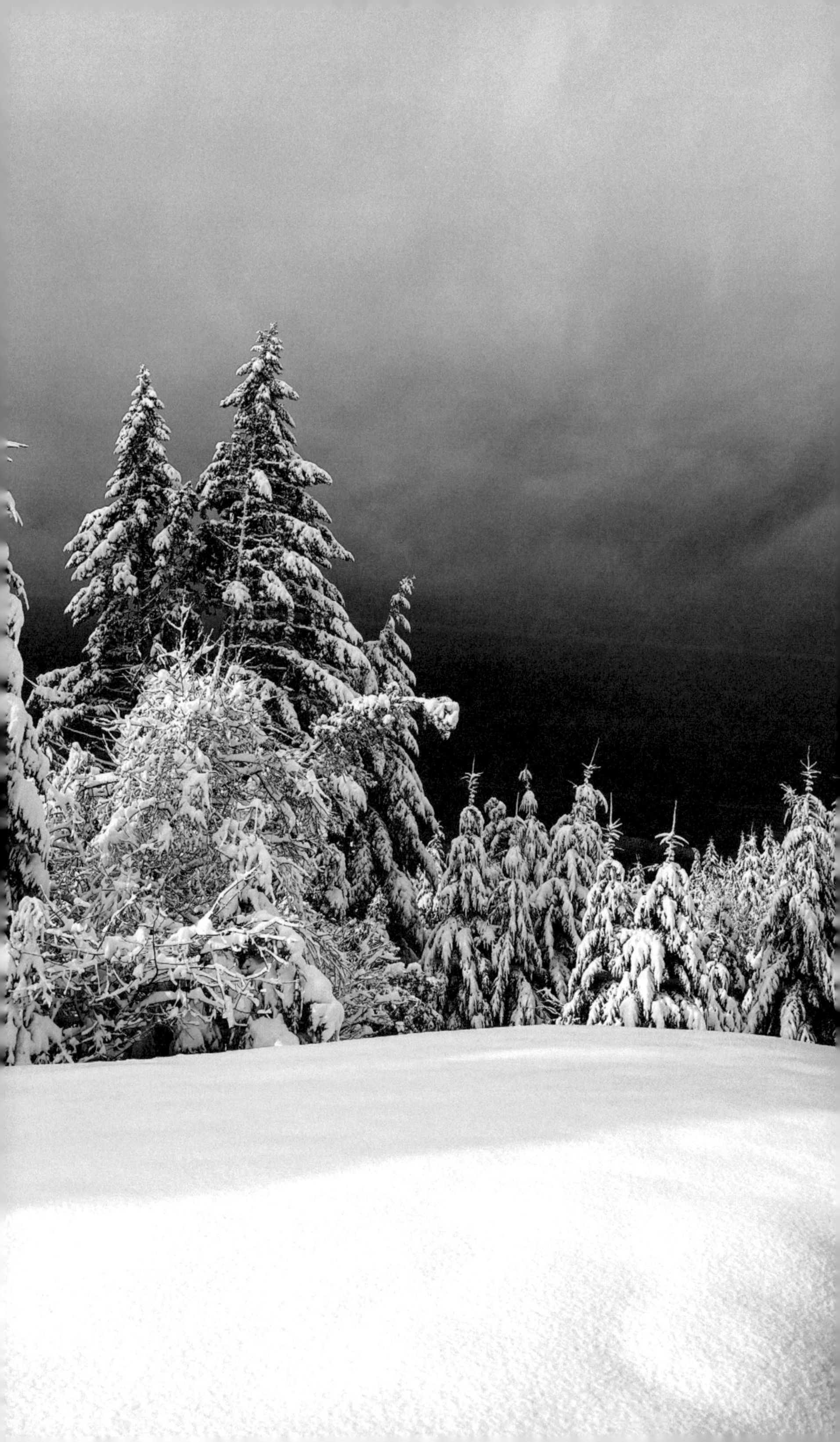

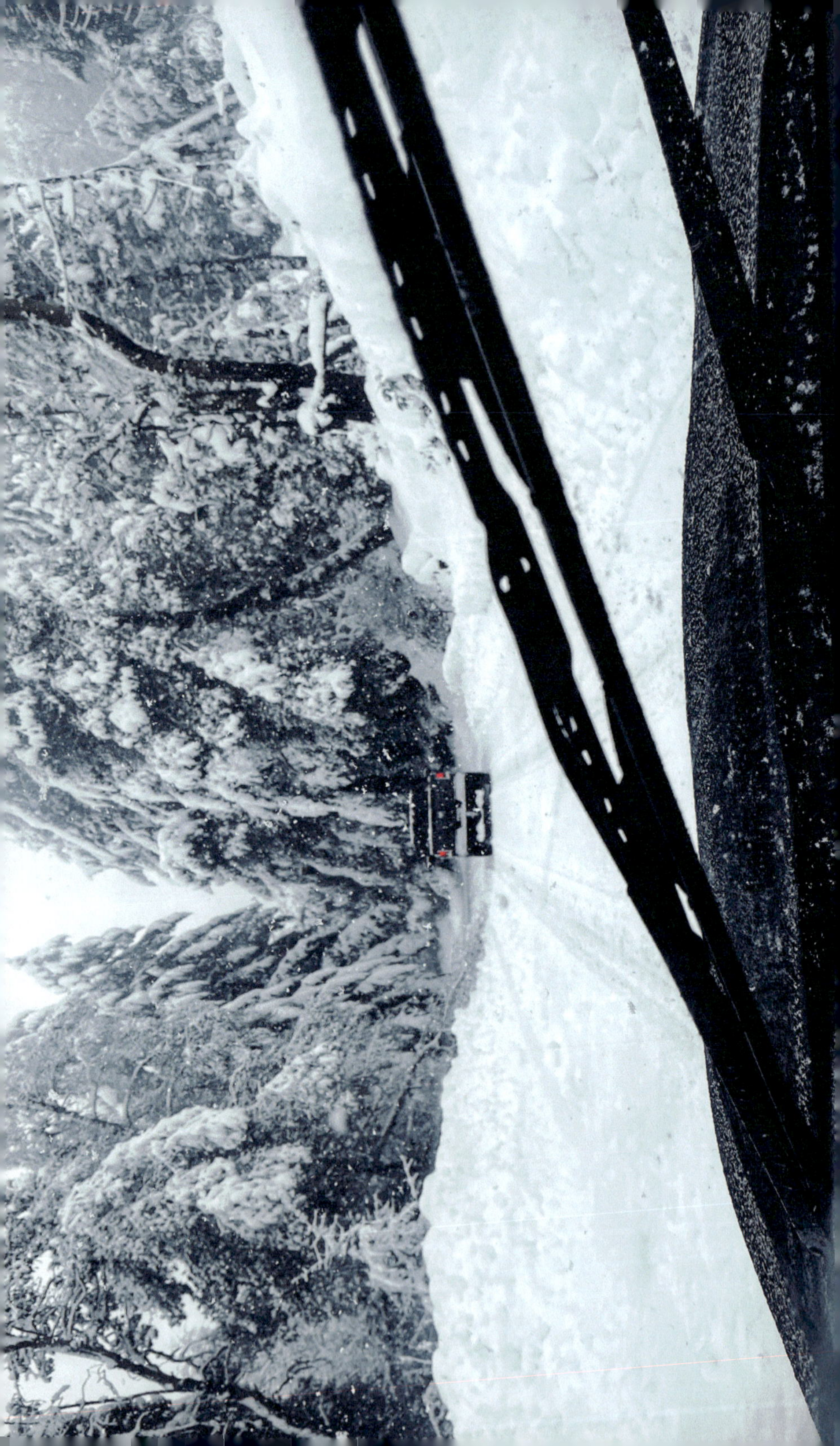

Miss Doe tracks

Snow + rain = ice

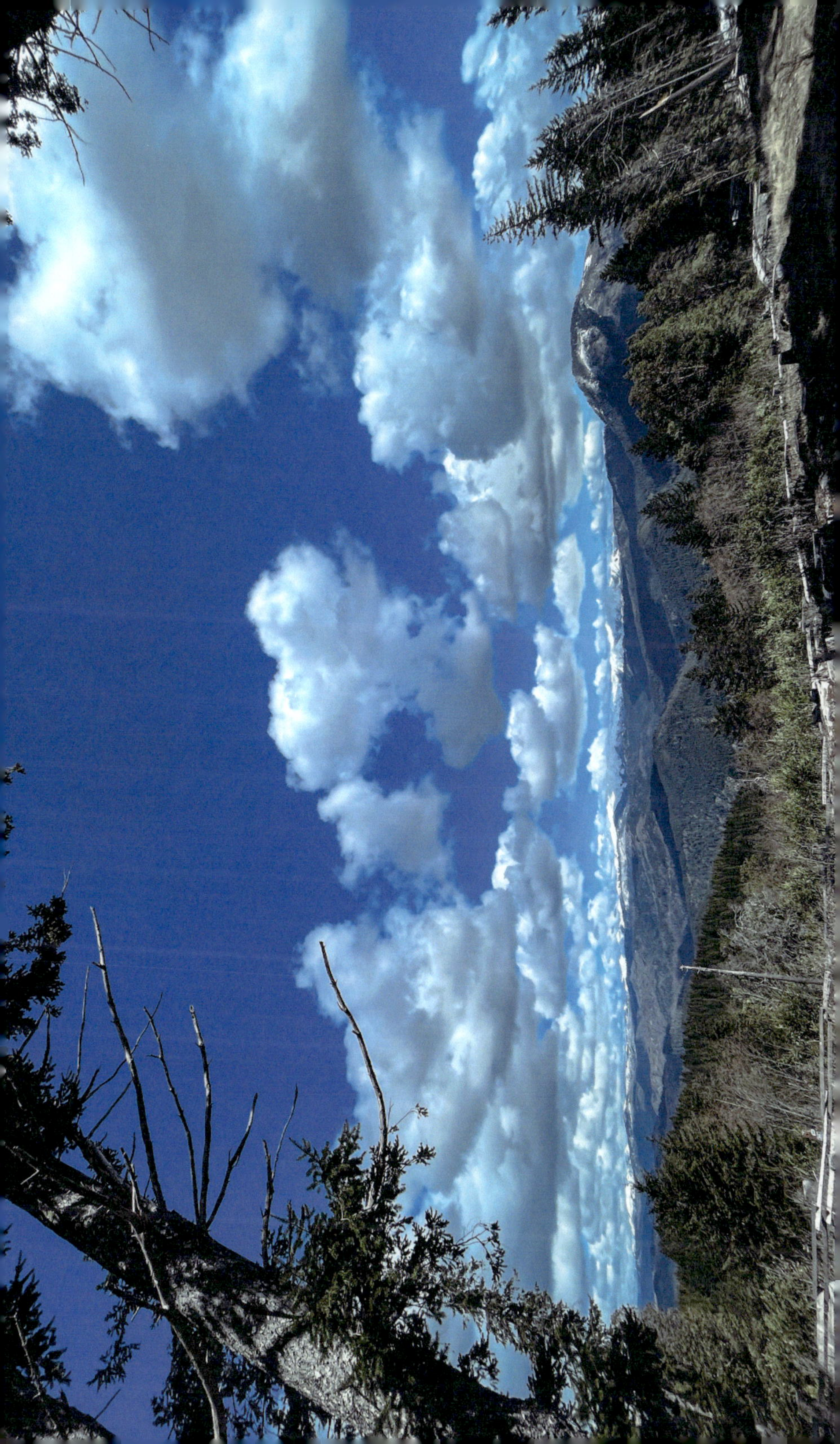

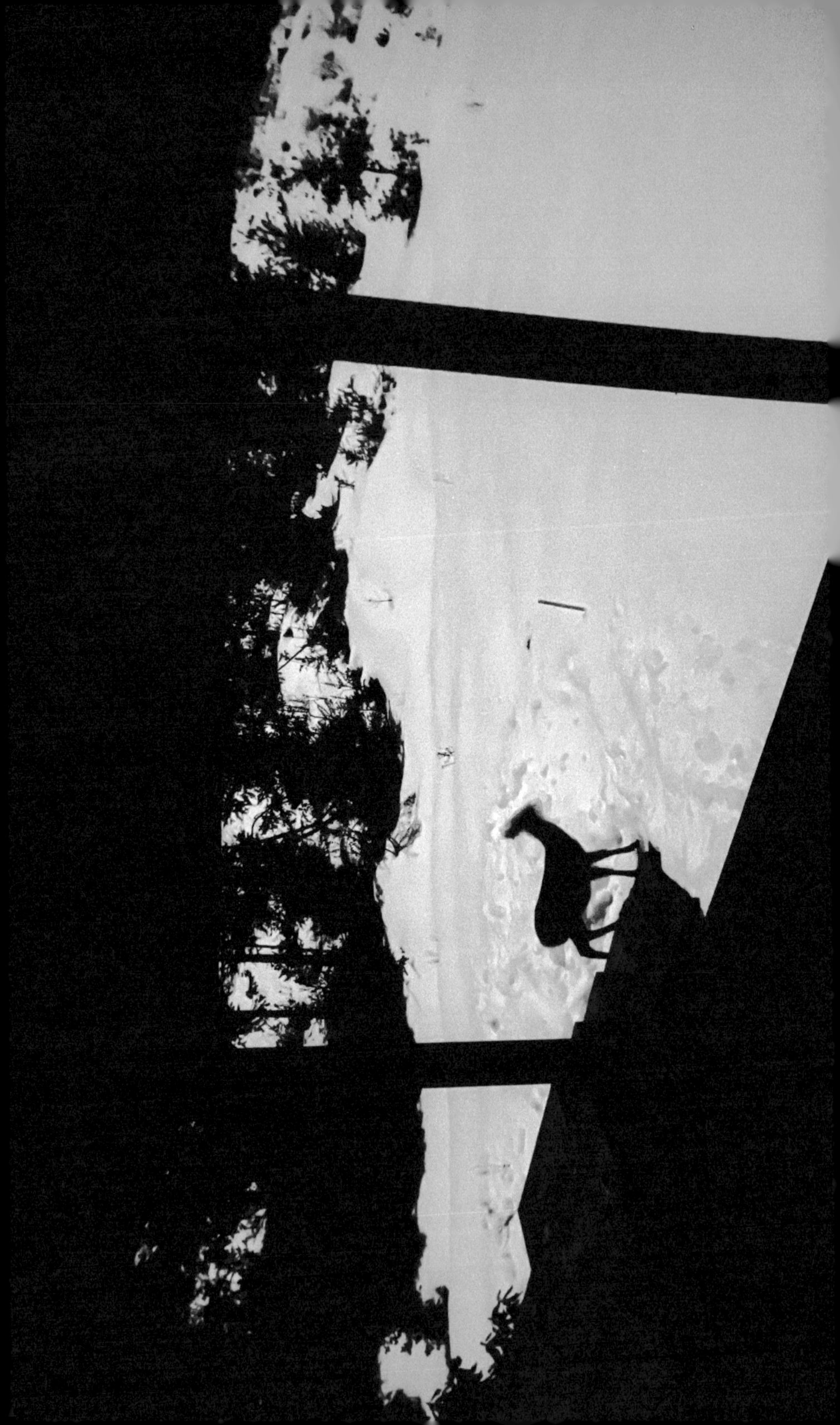

Chetco Cove

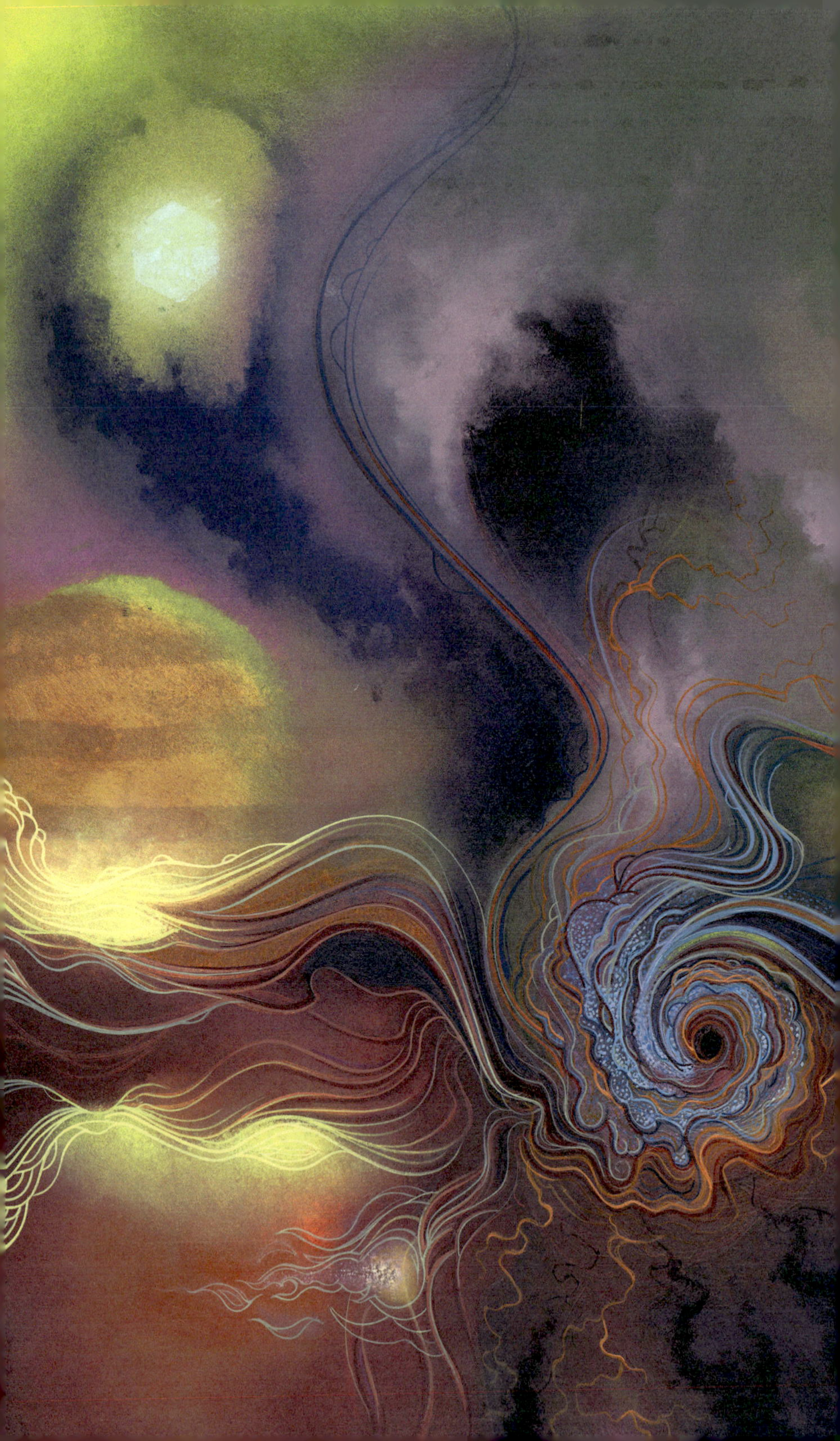

FLOWER PHOENIX

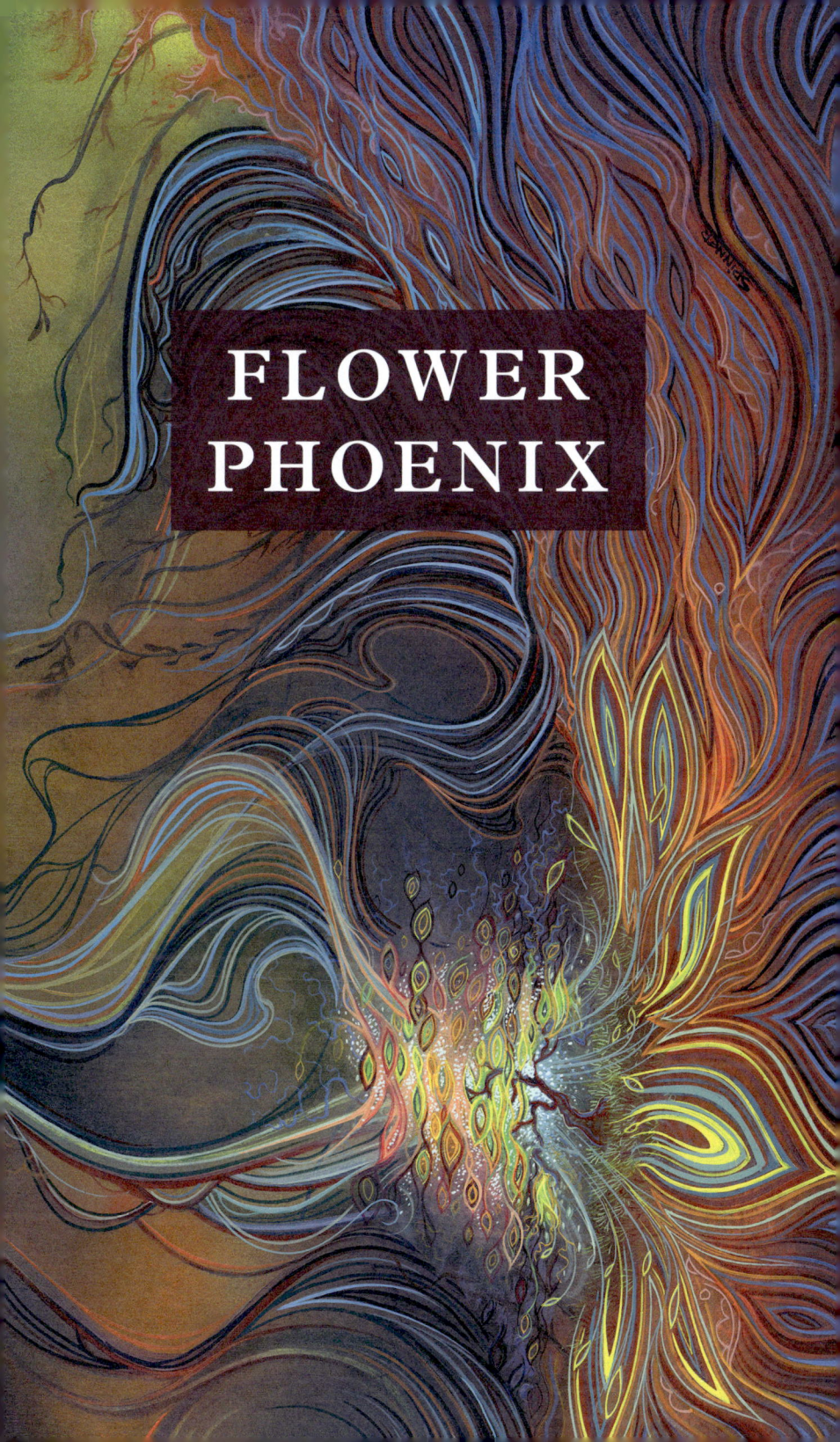

Rains of Holy Week. The snows of Tax Day. Smelted skies hermetically sealed. No Pink Moon moods. Again a southern Oregon coast April as wet wing of winter. Mercurial light fights lights of the alive. No bees, no blooms, no butterflies, no botanical beatniks. Deciduous souls: red alder, bigleaf and vine maple, hazel, cascara, lichen-laced white oak—all bare and asleep weeks deep into this extended chill.

But there be murmurs. Cozy sanct of a warm rain without wind. An agreeable surf day—a raft of sea lions slowly lists south, scattering gulls to the ambient drift. Clouds split—silhouetting western ridges, bristling with firs, a topaz sunset saturates the innocence of froggy dusk.

Easter upriver. Piercing rattlecall of a northern flicker on a tanoak fills the banshee void left by a varied thrush and a pileated woodpecker. He fled in the wee hour snow shower that cracked into another fog-dripped dawn swelling around secret misty mysteries. The center of my mind reverberates with the woodpecker's siren, his wild provincial cry split by resonant heartful drumming establishing his territory. His third consecutive spring here shrieking to mate, hammering down on that old hollow crooked madrone.

Murmurs—Aprilese.

And windows.

Rebirthese.

Hollow—the opening—maybe an equinoctial metaphor—time prying warmth from the cave of frost—new hopeful leafiness looming—softening balming of air and my attitude.

Since late January I've drawn weekly drives in the large white diesel pickup owned by my neighbors who are away for three months. They asked me to maintain their truck. So I do.

Another roady fling to peel eyes to the higher Sun. I zoom past lurks of dirty snow in dim crannies. The two paved lanes thread miles of dense unnaturally uniform Douglas-fir stands (units) of varying age. When a unit is left to grow approx 40 years up from seedling the site will be slain for local sawmills. Then replanted. Cyclical industrial monoculturing since the harmoniously diverse areal forests—many of them redwood— were last century leveled.

Elsewhere conifers were granted by white man and his frantic wildfire suppression. Fir seeds quickly spread across windy slopes. Land-clearing was unneeded per millennia of wildfire and indigenous care. Wide fertile upland Coast Range prairies and meadows were convenient canvases throughout the lower Chetco River watershed. Hence modern map misnomers Stump Prairie—Horse Prairie—Yank Prairie—Lookingglass Prairie—Northern Prairie—Mislatnah Prairie—High Prairie— Long Ridge Prairie—Quail Prairie. None now true prairies to the naked eye. Rich erstwhile habitats a checkerboard of sterile South Coast Lumber (SCL) plantations and Bureau of Land Management/National Forest swaths featuring overwhelmingly young- and middle-aged fir stands, covert tree farms themselves far removed from the virgin yorescapes of Curry County.

Earth Day. Atop Nook Creek's concave once-lush watershed I park the truck on a gravel logging road. Squint into a daylit mode of astral trinity—Sun, deep lagoon of sky, its cloudreef whites mirroring my far islands of thought.

Flecked with black snags and stumps and five-year-old firs lays the flaxen post-snow-smashed grass of Wilson Prairie. The grass looks sad but the stumps sadder. They elicit Kerouac and one of his many *Big Sur* anthropomorphisms: "The tree stumps say 'We are the tree stumps torn out of the ground by men sometimes by wind, we have big tendrils full of earth that drink out of the earth.'"

Here in April of epochs past were many tendrils but few if any stumps. There were wide undulations folding down into redwooded canyons and up to raw distant peaks and ridges draining the heavy winter rains and snowmelts nourishing infinities of pollen and nectar, of green wind-kissed brome and thistle urging winged singers and buzzings in crystal winds, and purple lupine and irises were popping and manzanitas bursting and tiny blue petals blinking in the bristling ceanothus. There were huge soarings of raptors over green seas of prey, avian song as reverie, bears and elk and deer grazing in edenic afternoons. It was all happening. All dripping from an opening in deep natural time.

Speaking of. The month's name may have stemmed from the Latin *Aprilis* which was the second month in Rome's ancient calendar, *Aprilis* culled from the also-Latin *aperire* ("to open"). Circa 6 CE, Roman grammarian Verrius Flaccus created the *Praenestini*, an elaborate inscribed *fasti* (calendar) stating that, in April, "the fruits and flowers and animals open up, both by sea and by land."

At Wilson Prairie too last spring I'd puzzled over human intrusion in biodiversities and industrial historicals, ecosystems of supplies and demands, of weather averages, of unnatural natures in reverse that suddenly were in fact stopped and jerked forward, reopened—freed—by fire.

Lightning-lit, that fire (Chetco Bar—191,197 acres, July-September 2017) spent most of its its life on public lands, from the roadless heart of Kalmiopsis Wilderness out to within five miles of Brookings. Before the fire was fully contained, Curry County Commissioner Court Boice waxed hyperbolic at a community meeting. "It's absolute, immeasurable devastation," he told the crowd. "We just lost 200,000 acres of some of the best land in the state of Oregon."

Lost?

In the end Chetco Bar left a mixed-severity burn mosaic of which 98 percent thankfully has been left alone. Within a year though in these precise abused earths beneath my feet, every inch of affected SCL land (1,868 acres) and 2,222 acres (slimmed from the proposed 13,626 of which 9,000 were wild intact never-logged ecosystems) of affected National Forest in the lower Chetco watershed were completely and prematurely scalped in a contentious blitzkrieg euphemized as "salvage logging."

Inadvertently for SCL was the unveiling of a huge slumbering golden antidote. Oceans of herbaceous seed and rhizome asleep for decades, sealed by heavy equipment and Douglas-fir plantations and resultant duff, were at last liberated to burst like diamonds into the sunlit air. Native shrubs shot from archipelagos of old roots. Large dreamy meadows were phoenixed, the flames fissuring and combusting perverse grove uniformities, unleashing colorful frenzies of old, resetting an ancient ecological clock.

Briefly.

Arbor Day. Midmorning. The past few days have bled a blast of fantastic warmth. Highest temps since October. Air without edges. The land and wildlife slowly reopen. At dusk a female cougar has prowled and chirped and screeched for a mate in the healing woods below my home.

Again I rumble the neighbors' truck up onto the logging roads wefting through reborn coastal prairies. After the 2018 salvage logging, sadly, all were promptly replanted only to be (barring another fire) clearcut in about 40 years. Today many of the new firs are up to my ribs amongst low groves of new manzanita and last year's brown flattened grass. The new grass is still just an inch or two high and wildflowers remain dormant. Because of consistent cold and snow, everything is late.

Dry northeast breeze shooshes through the baby trees and melts the late snows from distant brooding bulges of the Kalmiopsis—Vulcan Peak, Chetco Peak, Red Mountain. Worshipful Sun soaks into my face—ears are soothed by the familiar comfort twee of a spotted towhee, the sweet whist of whitecrown sparrows, trill of juncos, squeaky *kee-aah* of a red-shouldered hawk gliding and scanning above the giggling tributaries of Panther Creek.

What's lost is found and will again be lost and found. To humans, both are subjective. That's the bough and the bloom and the brome. The forever biome where roots converse. All of this amongst valuable debris of burnt snags and logs. A lost landscape found in transition.

Atop a blackened stump I find a manzanita inflorescence that could be mistaken as a chewed piece of pink bubble gum. The tiny bell-shaped flowers smell of soft perfume. Oddly placed there by something winged or clawed. Or the wind. Or a spring flower fairy. We can all use one of those.

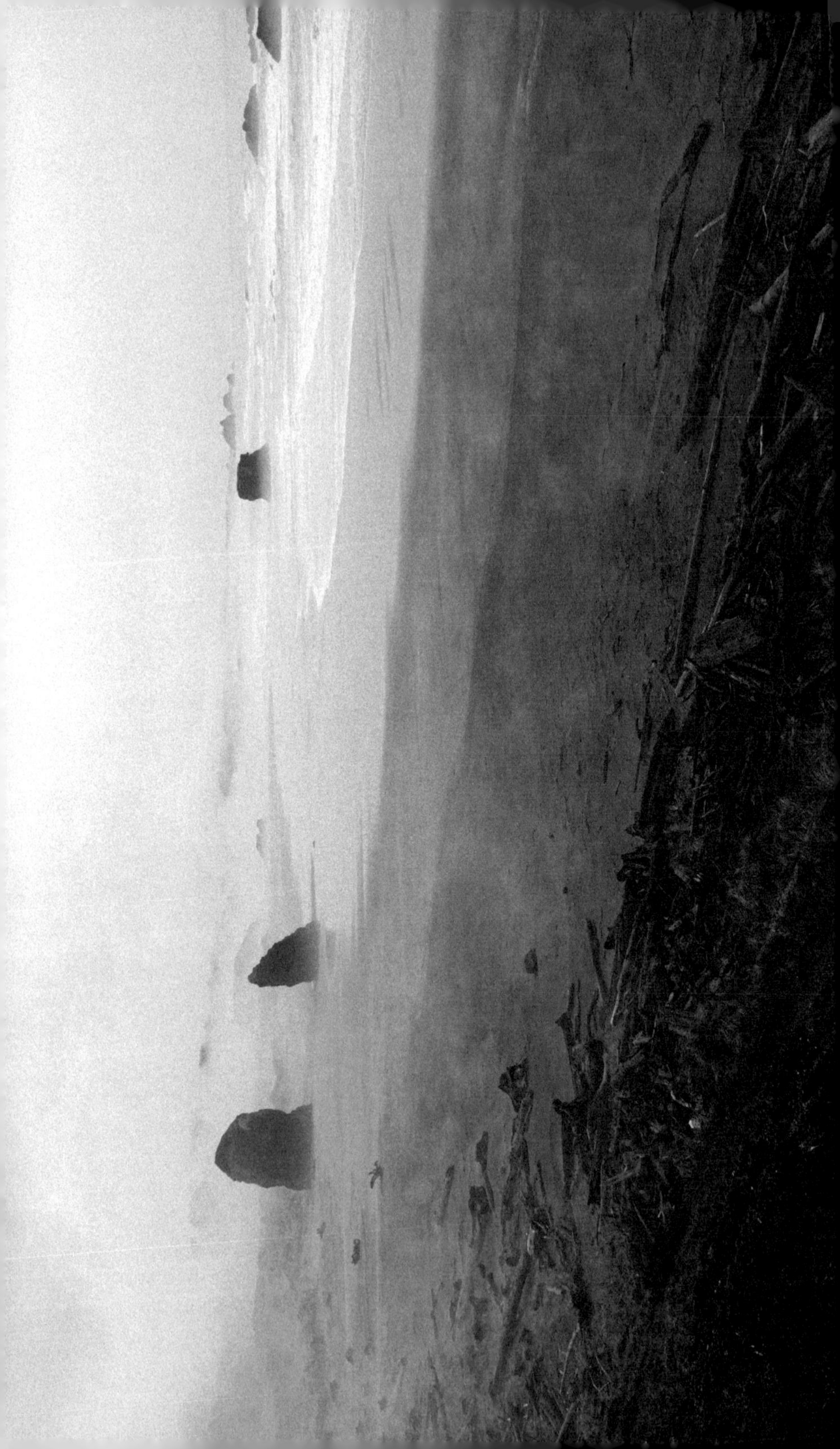

Meyers Creek Beach

Mill Beach

Chetco River

Bosley Butte

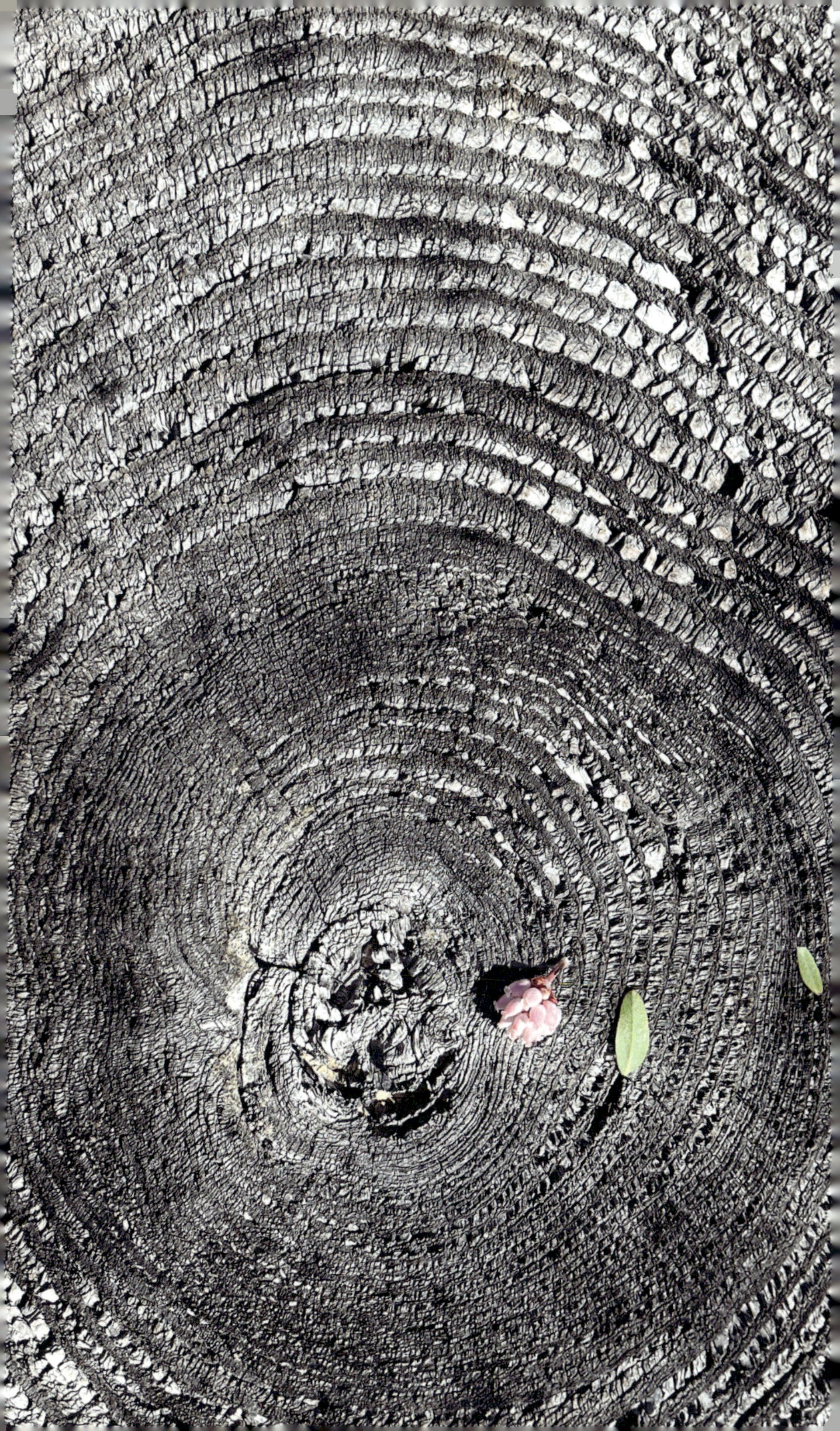

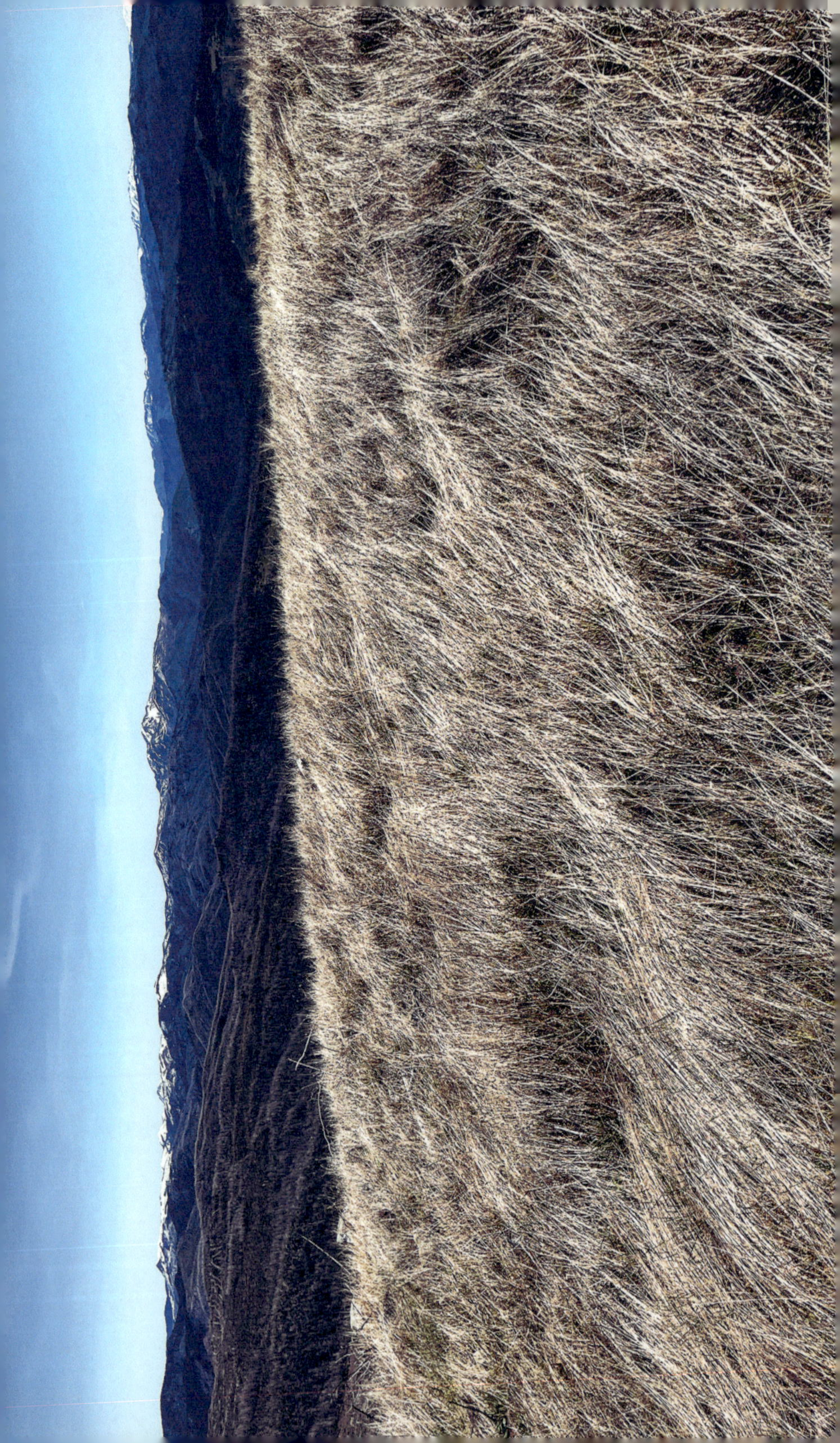

Pink Moon over Mount Emily

"Salvage logging" clearcuts below Quail Prairie

Douglas-fir

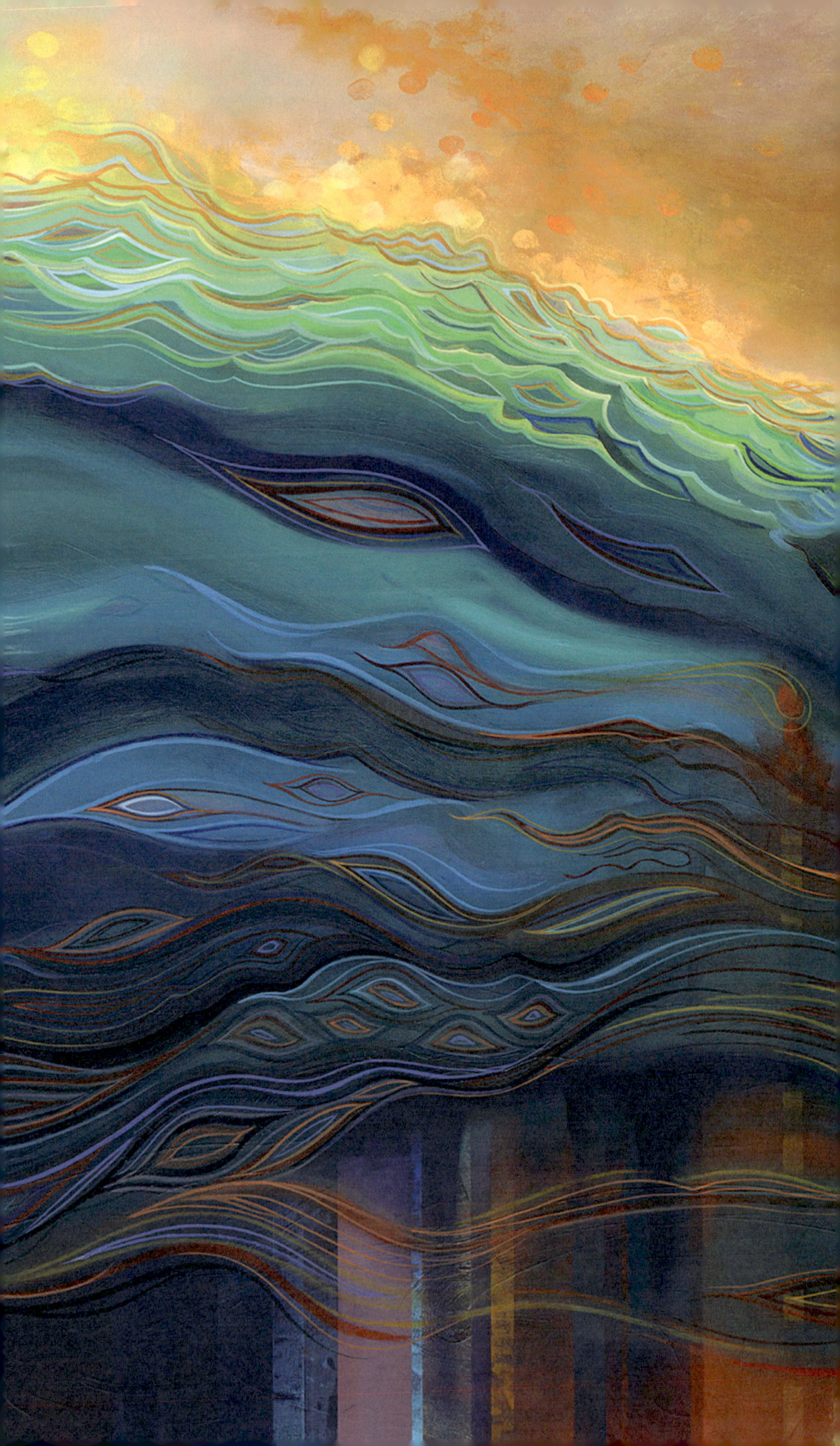

THE KINS OF MAY

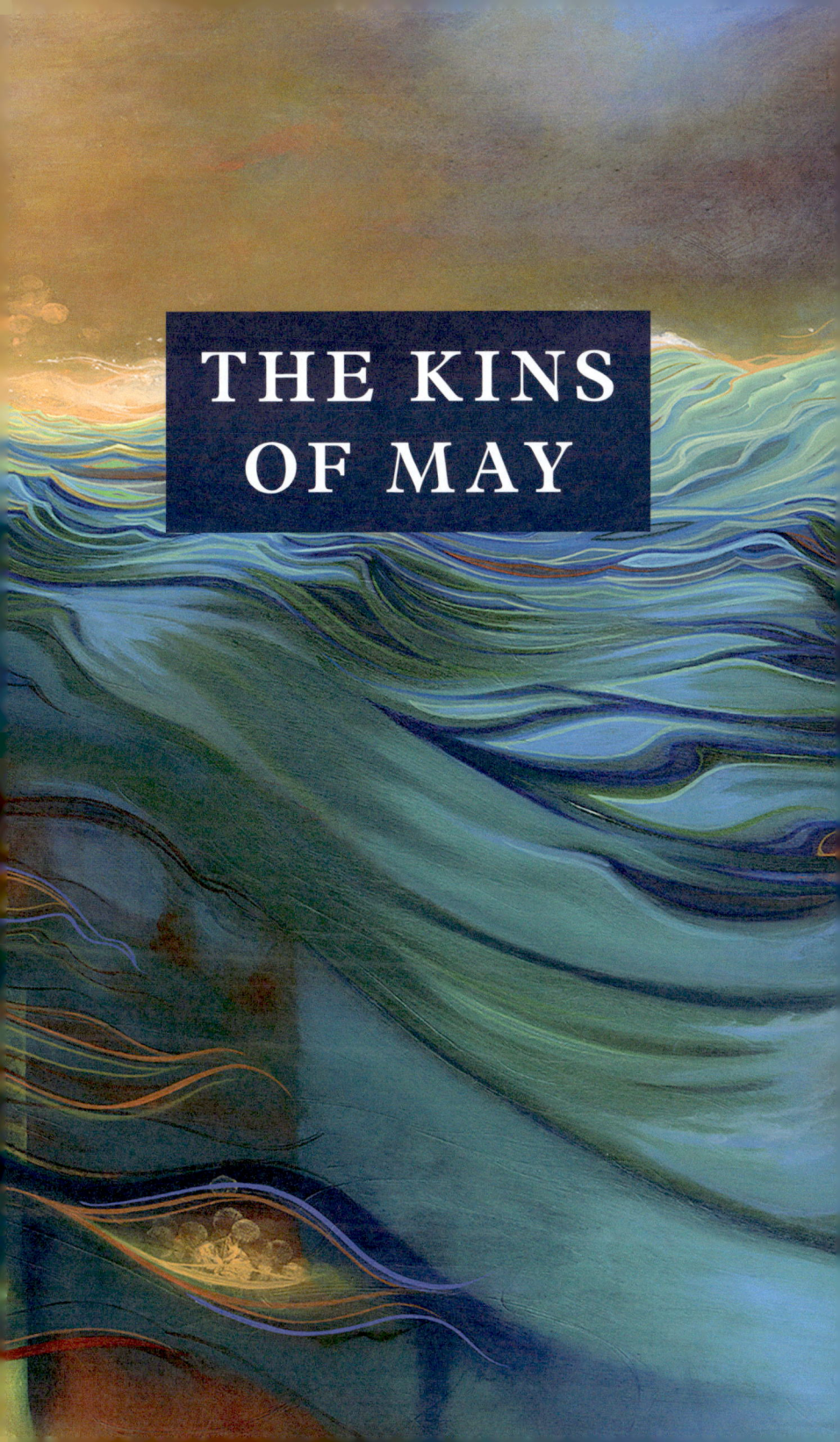

And out here swings May Day, a-bluster in billow and grayrainy tumult linking the world's hopeful eyes to Beltane, eve of my smiling father's 80th, his years on Earth laid bare here at the cold foot of spring.

And I am the King of May, which is the power of sexual youth—

And with whole family in his choice restaurant we sip champagne and carouse. Celebrating the wheel of impermanence.

With soup my dementic mother sits quietly. Through my father's dreams and love spawned her mirrored heartbeat of my Bohemian ancestry. Hanzlik. Maternal pedigree swooshing and stumbling from deep Czech to secret Salish, a blond braid burnt and twisted across frozen lakes and Rockies and Coast Range, my forefathers' glowing Slavic embers an inferno in the green gem rainforest, its May mycelia eventually spidering south like flowers of future fortune.

And of course up there hides the dusky full Flower Moon amid its penumbral eclipse above modern southOregon mists that finger the sweet valleys and skullcap their snowy peaks. Was a Czech polarity 53 years prior—the also-invisible NEW Moon swung away from poet/provocateur Allen Ginsberg as he goofed there in '65 amid Iron Curtain travels after his expulsion from Cuba at the height of Cold War.

And I am the King of May, which is long hair of Adam and the beard of my own body—

During the historically free-spirit youthFest of Majáles (first in 20 years) he was cardboard-crowned as the honorable May Day King by cheery beery polytechnics and paraded up

Soviet-bloc Communists and Nazis that were soiling and poisoning minds (1966's Fest plunged into a riot).

And I am the King of May, in a giant jetplane touching Albion's airfield trembling in fear—

London-bound on May 7, Ginsberg poeticized, documenting his strange quasiroyal Czech interlude. Two weeks earlier my parents had wed in northern California. Ten+ years later I was delivered and middle-named Hanzlik to preserve my queenmother's vein.

And I am the King of May, which is old Human poesy, and 100,000 people chose my name—

Before revisiting Prague (his first trip fell in March) Ginsberg probed his maternal dirt in and around Moscow. Sent to America in 1905, same year an official Mother's Day was conceived, Naomi Ginsberg (née Levy) would later sag from severe psychosis, living in mental hospitals and gifted a lobotomy. Slain by a stroke in '56, same year Allen published *Howl*, an epic to me and millions—*I saw the best minds of my generation destroyed by madness—*

And flown in upon a 91°F heatwave swoops here the crystal American silence of Mother's Day. Through the months from her diagnosis, mine speaks less and less. Fragments, confusions, her once-clear best-mind-of-generation sky slowly clouding, numbing. A Hanzlik heaven that rains tears for the rest of us. A Flower Moon wilting.

A Bohemian queen forced inward.

Outward meanwhile a few queens survived winter. Spermed last autumn and now freed from dormancy to nectarize and nest-build in the eaves and feed and breed teeming families of worker wasps. All in time for the seas of ruby rhododendrons and purple irises to bloom and for me to emotionally tune for my precious and dearly beloved Marvin (17yo tuxedo cat) to cross over his rainbow bridge.

More lights of impermanence.

And in bright Memorial Day summerflower warmth I wail about and squeeze heartpain of this sacred spring and feed and breed my own teeming rainbow-mind mycelia through the cold holy body of pilsner, ancestral chemistry blessed from the city of Plzeň (aka Pilsen) and its zen valleys of fertility.

Plzeň is West Bohemia's soul. Pilsner Urquell was my go-west grandfather's go-to. In his own way he too was a king of May. As is my father dearest. As is Marvin. My muse who loves beer. But our real choices? Those we don't make? All that's well and good in life will forever start with queens. And sunshine dreams. And remember always—always—with your closest kin of smiling sheen.

Chetco River

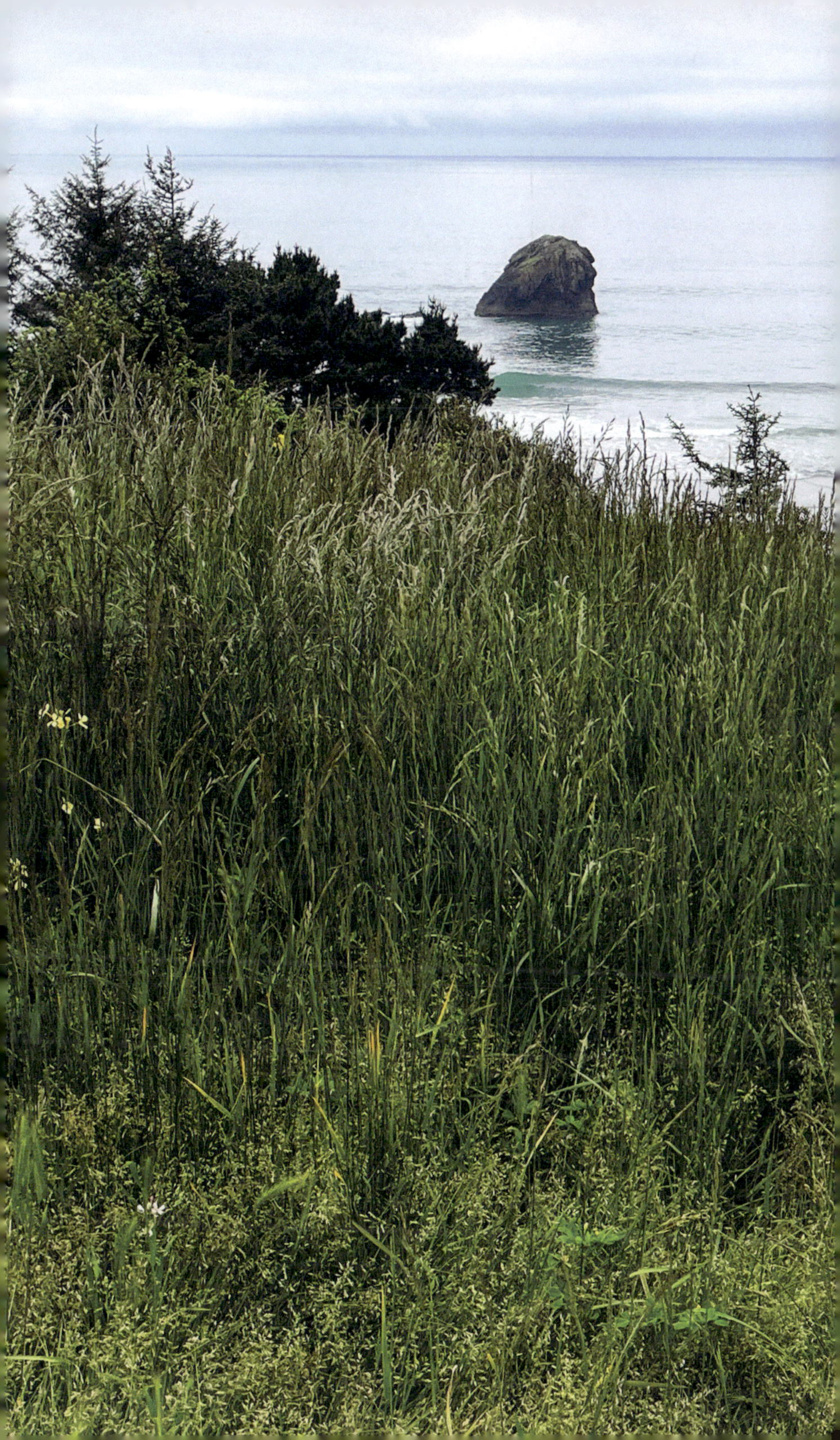

Rosey rhododendrons

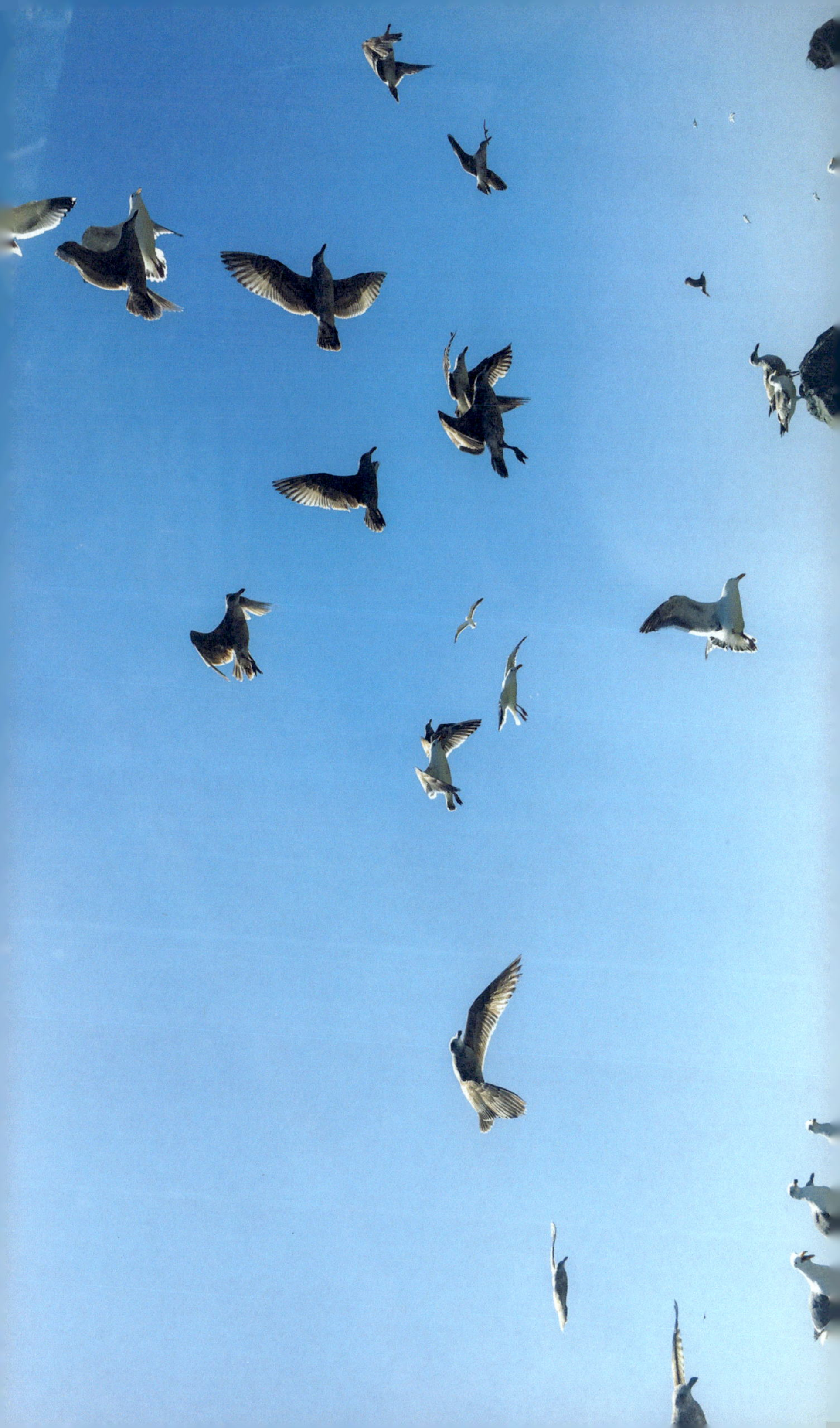

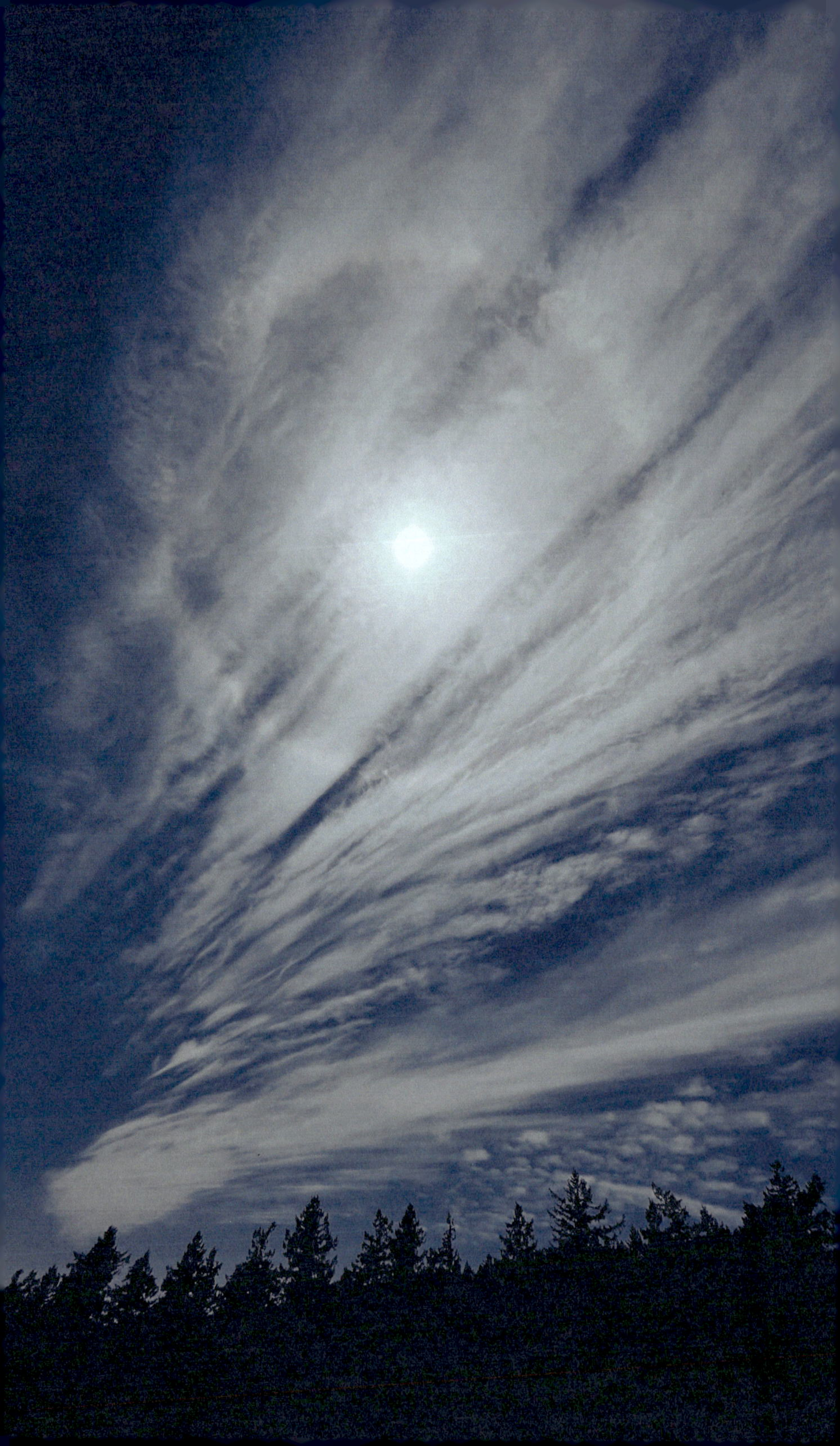

AG in Prague. Photo: Karel Syrp, courtesy Allen Ginsberg Estate

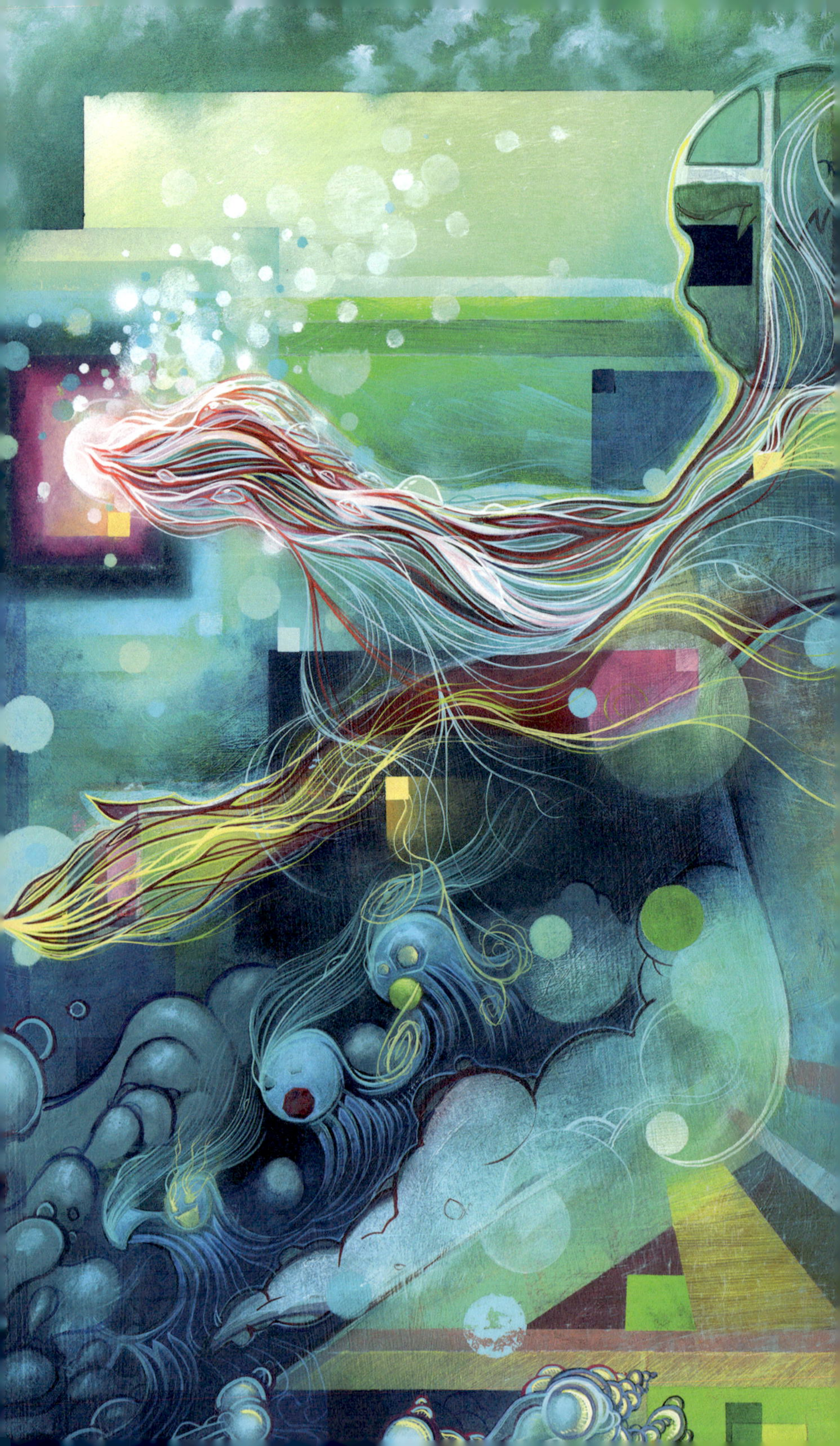

THE TIME WE CARRY

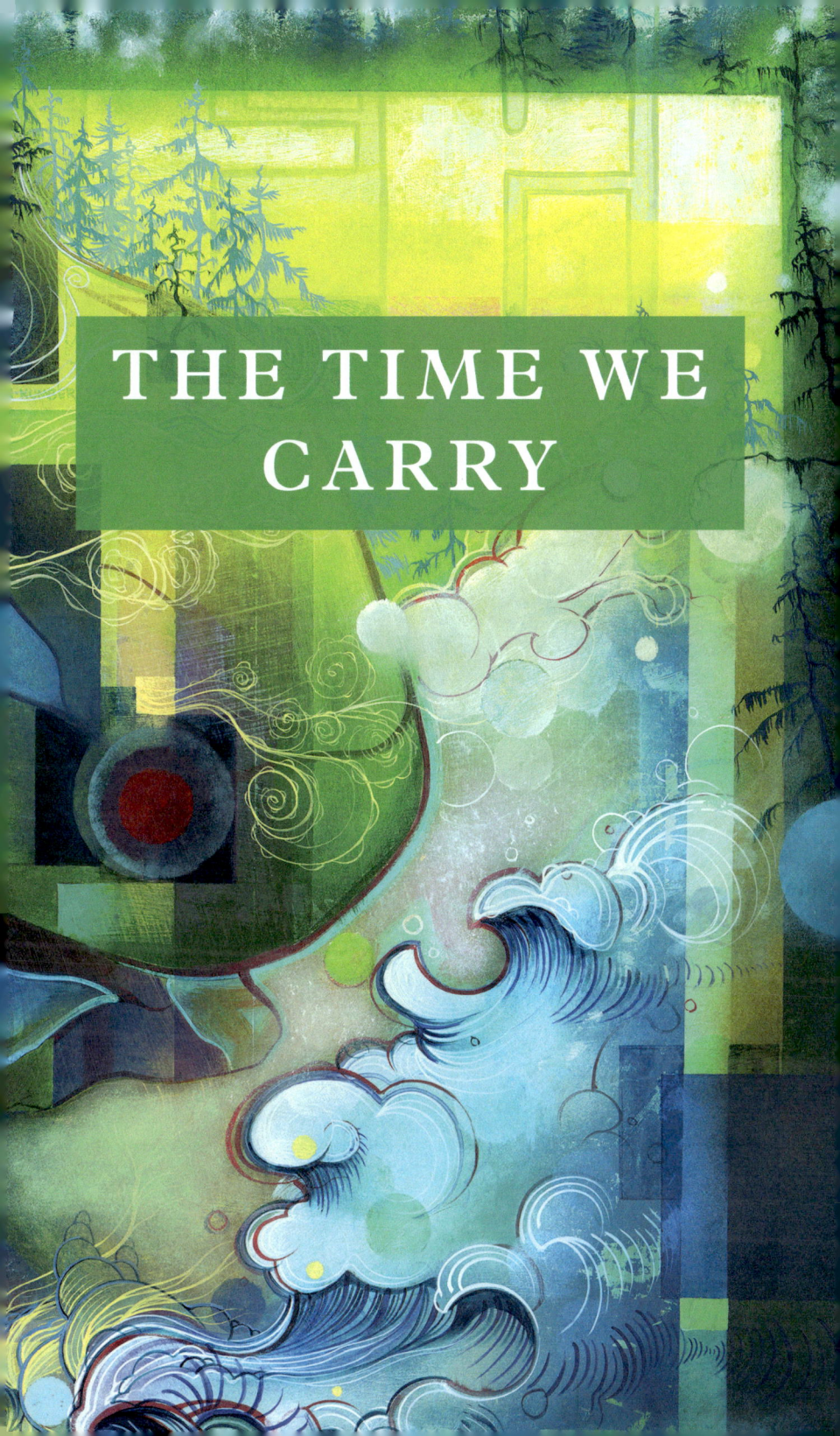

In summer you walk often. Walk out to walk in. You carry things. The solstice carries you.

I carry a white single-fin. From my 47-year-old trapezius hangs a black 28-liter wet/dry bag. Tool for bipedal surf-search. Fitted with tick-blocking pants and day-hikers, 7'0" underarm, I step down through a ferny fen of huckleberry, salal, and wind-sheared spruce to this gap in the south Oregon coast.

Rocky, reefy, curvy. Google Earth porn.

You don't surf here. Except today. For the first time in two years. Perhaps two decades. Perhaps never. Perhaps never again.

Slow warming Sundazehaze slinks and numbs the afternoon, all soft-focus pastels that blur cirrus into a sea psychedelia.

Dreamtime.

Glass.

Look: gulls and seals and a spouting gray whale. Bobbing bulling kelp lazing in the drift, swaying with the surge, lacing with white ribbons of sea plasma. Depths of coldly fragrant-fresh jade blending with hillside groves. Sky whiffing of salt and soot. Offshore looming of sea stacks and tortured rocks, relics of this coast a billion years old.

My feet and 60,000 years of human pollination reach this beach. Primordial panoramas—beige strip of heavily driftwooded sand, coarse as cracked pepper, cloaked with cliff and forested secret.

By you I am unseen. Publicly private. Ephemeral refuge. Naturalist's zen. Church of the open sky.

I could be elsewhere.

Since Middle Paleolithic Homo sapiens left the Horn of Africa, we've walked. All of us. We've carried things. Our first portable sheath was likely a pelt quiver for arrows, freeing our hands to hunt and gather. After 45,000 years of peregrination, Alaska was reached and the East Asian pilgrims scattered, launching today's diaspora of Native Americans from Barrow to Ushuaia. They carried things too.

Bag things: steel bottle, energy bar, hooded five-mil. Modern rucksack gleans roots of 130 years. But in 1991 two German hikers found Ötzi the Iceman in an Italian Alps gully. Arteries split by a foe's flint-tipped arrow, he died 5,300 years prior, deer-hide quiver and wood frame beside him. Bits of hide and hair suggested a hide sack indeed was stuck to the frame.

Stone Age backpacking, you might say.

Whilst surfing I ponder Paul Salopek, a stranger whose dream I trace. Today he too is backpacking. Carrying things. Things to capture and share his global trek.

"Walking is falling forward," he told National Geographic a decade yore when the writer first faced the hot wind and dust of Herto Bouri. It was from here he'd launched his 21,000-mile Out of Eden Walk—"a journey that belongs to all of us"—exiting Ethiopia and threading the Middle East and eyeballing the ancient Silk Road, eventually to ford the North Pacific and descend the Americas to Tierra del Fuego, man's—and Salopek's—omega.

"(Out of Eden) is a recreation of a journey all of us have made if you just go far back enough in our family trees," he said. "It's going to press the boundaries of communicating in a world where there's too much information and not enough meaning. I'm going to swim upstream against the flow of information and try to slow people down, to have them absorb stories at a human pace."

Slow journalism.

Salopekinspiration?

Heavy into Year 10 of the Walk, he's angling through a bewitching China toward the burning beacon of Siberia, last stop before the Bering Strait and the rogue New World. Today's world.

From his 61-year-old trapezius hangs a communications kit (laptop, camera, notebook, cell/sat phone) so he can "fling open digital infinitudes our nomadic forebears could scarcely imagine . . . We've been wired by natural selection to absorb meaning from our days at the loose-limbed gait of three miles an hour."

Four-p.m. Sun balms my face. Slouched forward, spent from waveriding, I watch the creep of tide, the diurnal teaser, the surf session killer. The sandbar is dead—fleeting, like us. Estimates claim that 93 percent of all humans to ever live—more than 100 billion—are gone. Soul vapor. Bone dust.

Do you believe in atomic reincarnation?

Five ospreys squeak and twirl overhead—fish too will die. The ancient circle. Wheel of life.

I stand and reposition the bag. Grip the single-fin. Slowly from this beach I step from the past into the present, up through the foyer of rainforest, an old friend, rediscovering it, supplanting memory, carrying things one age to the next.

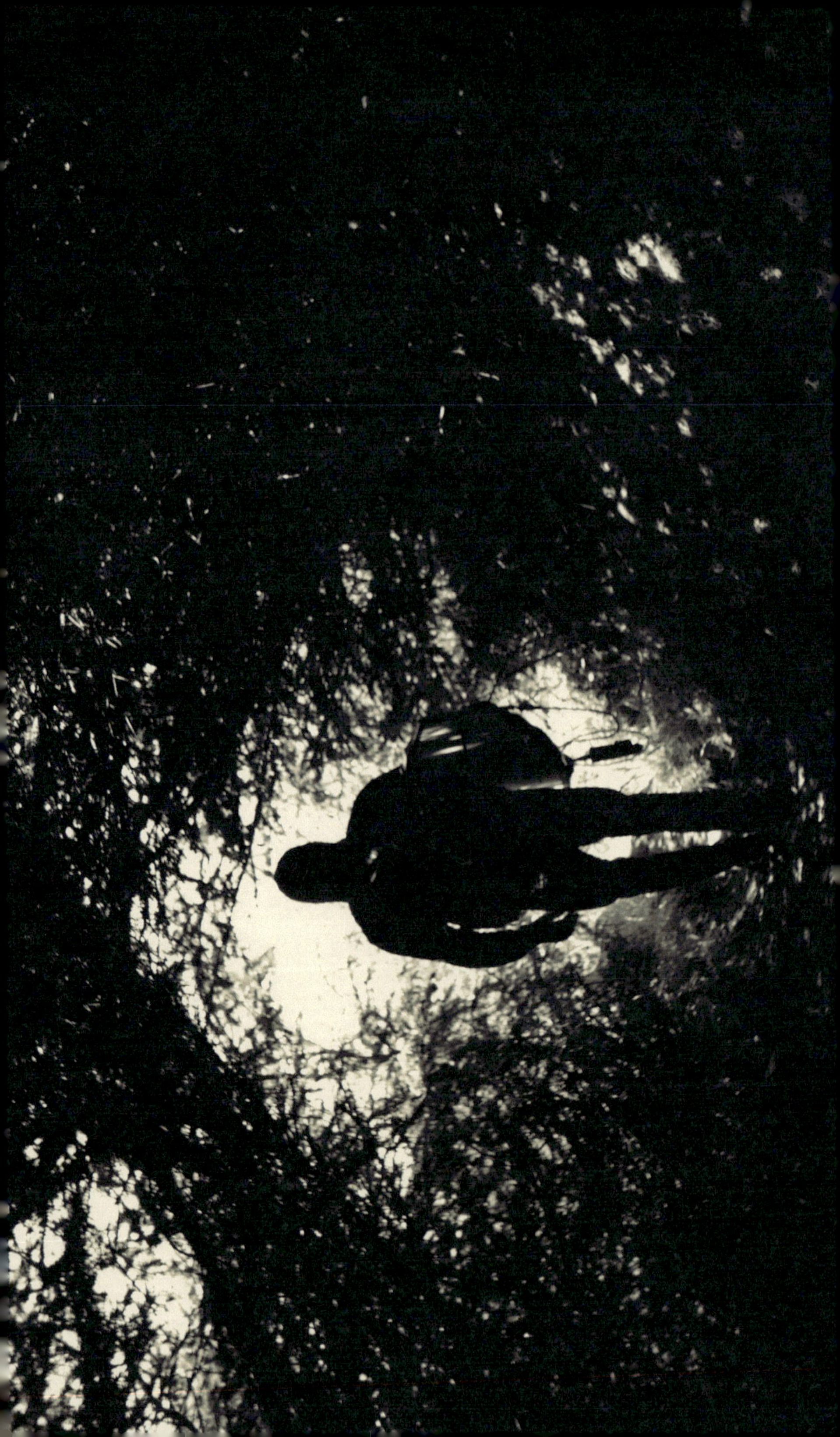

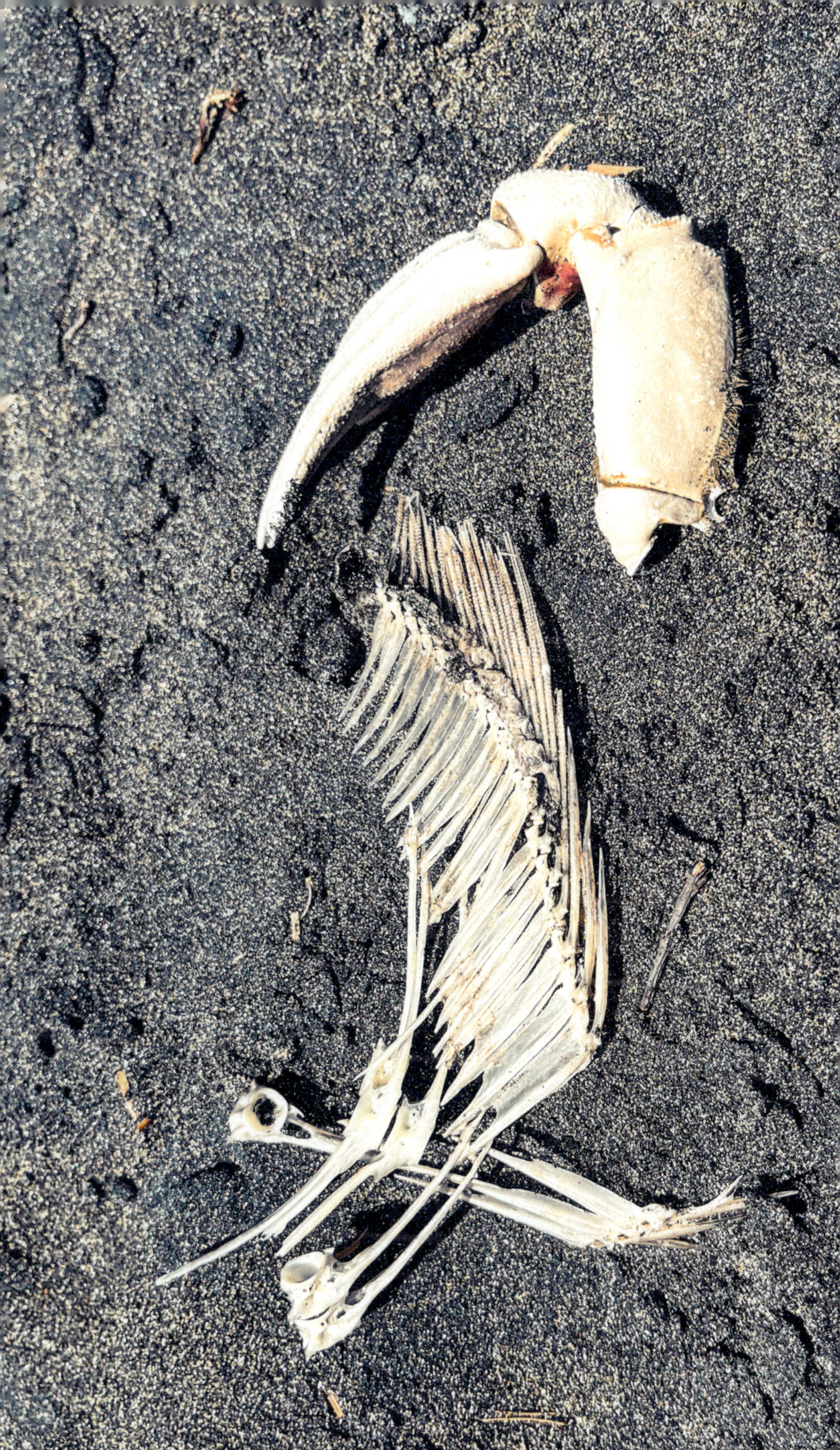

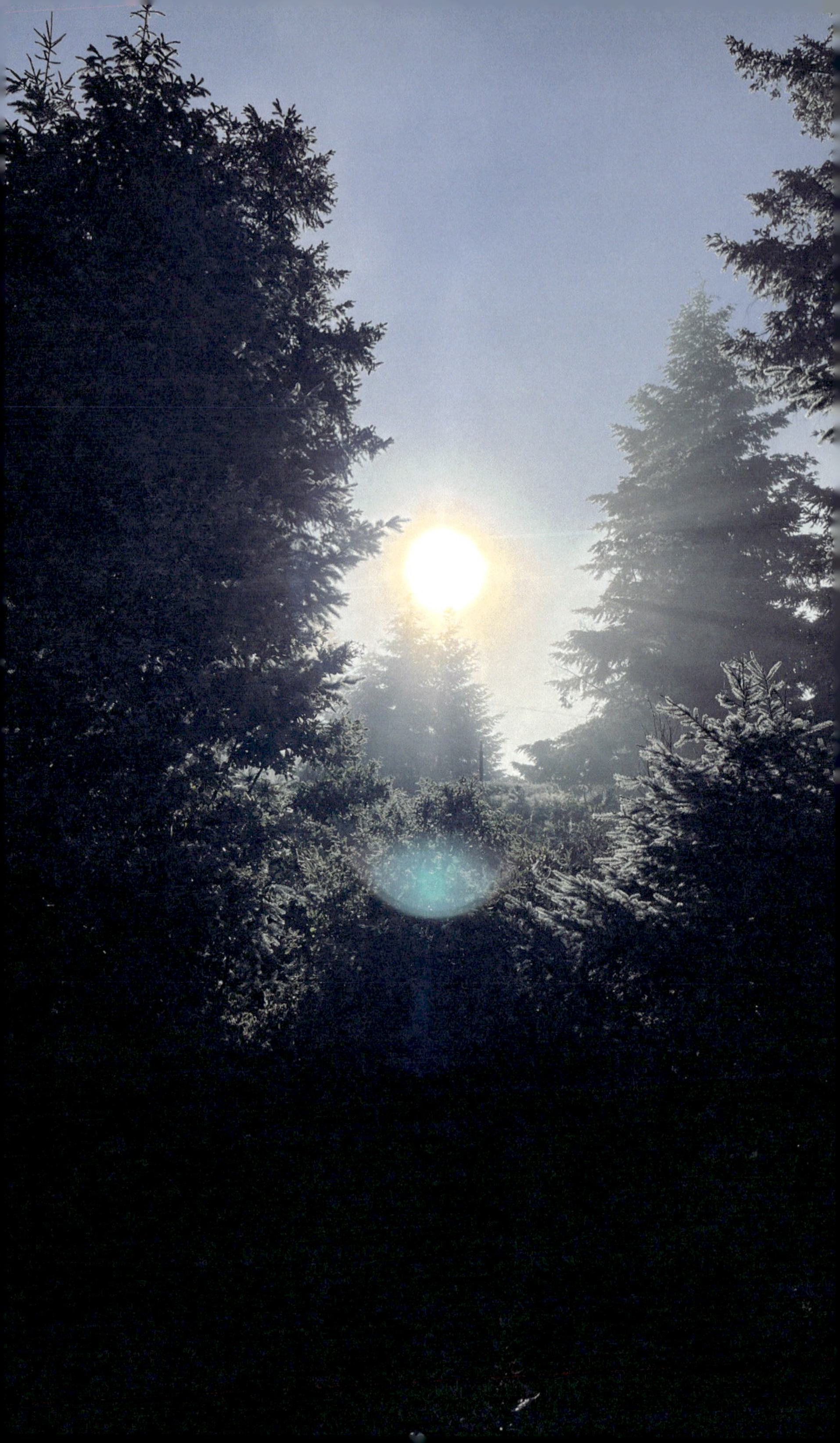

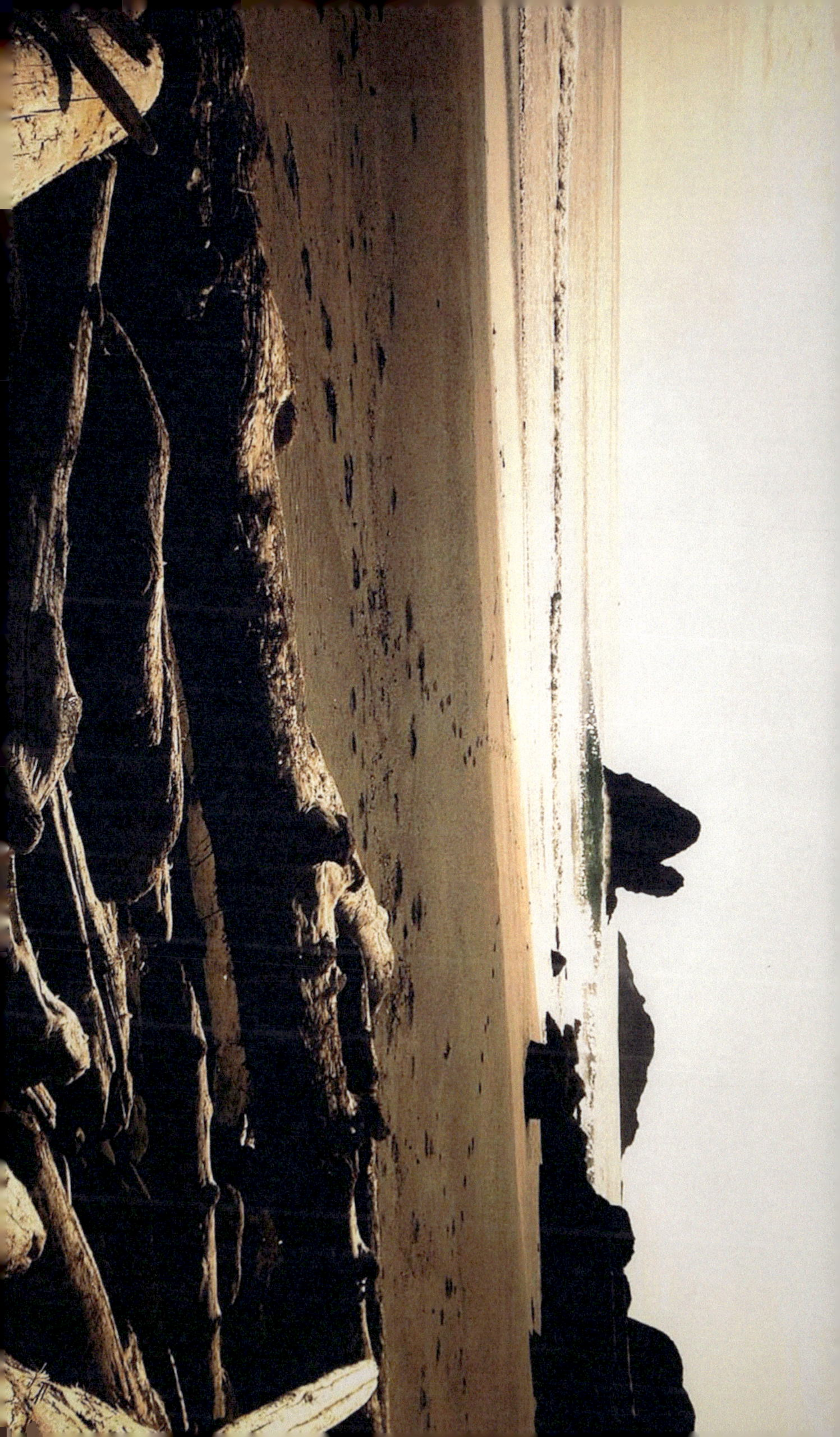

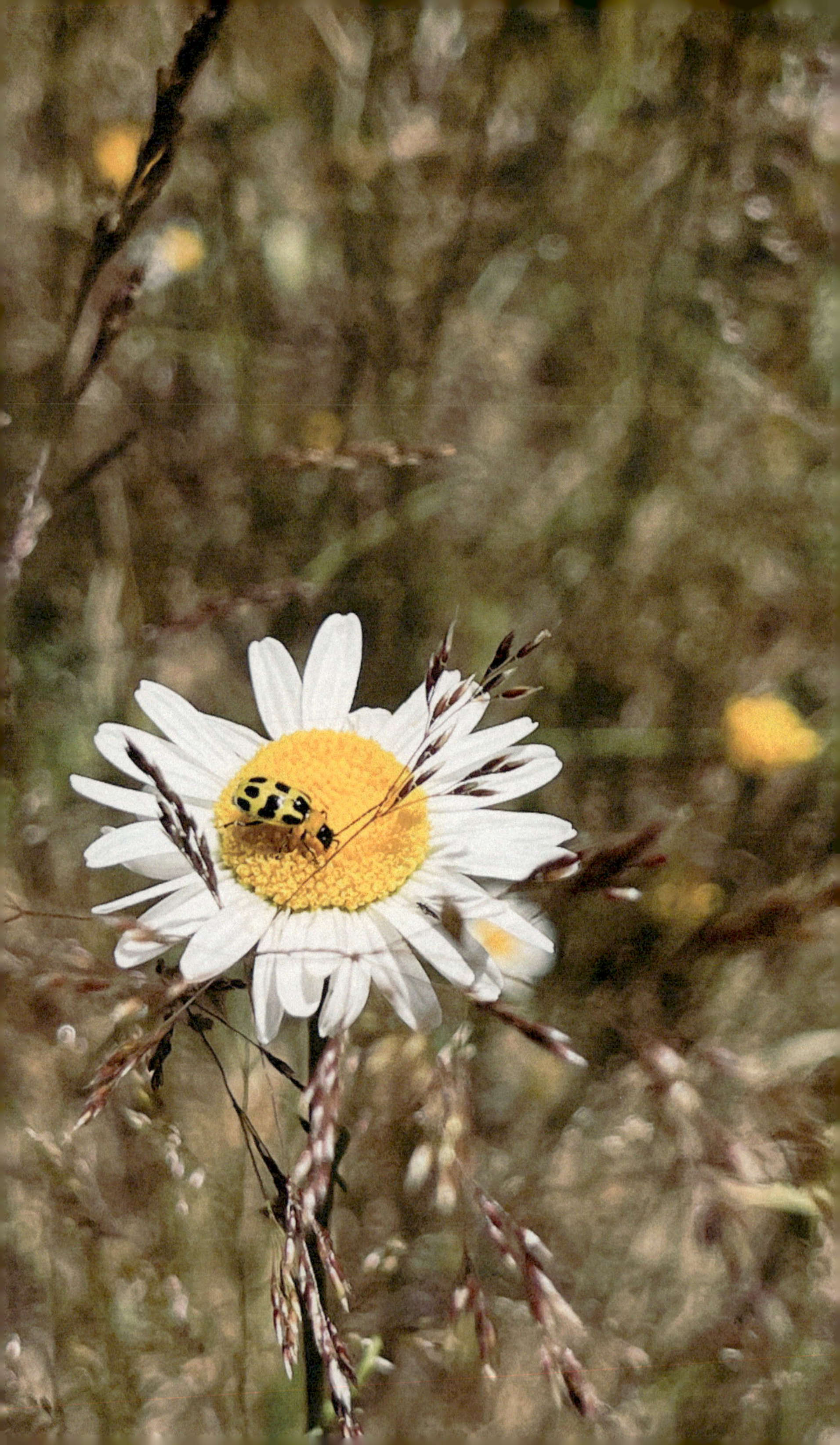

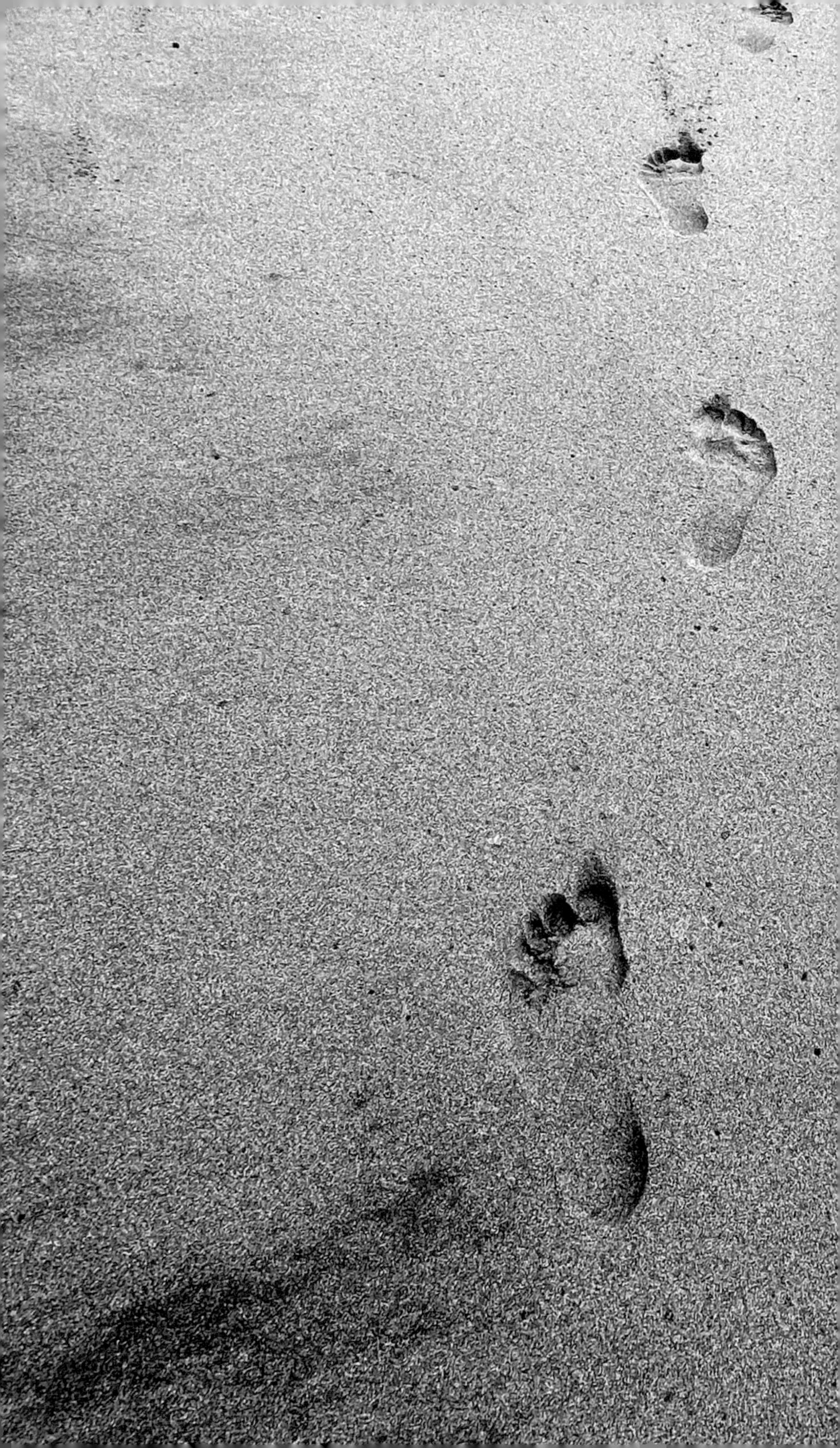

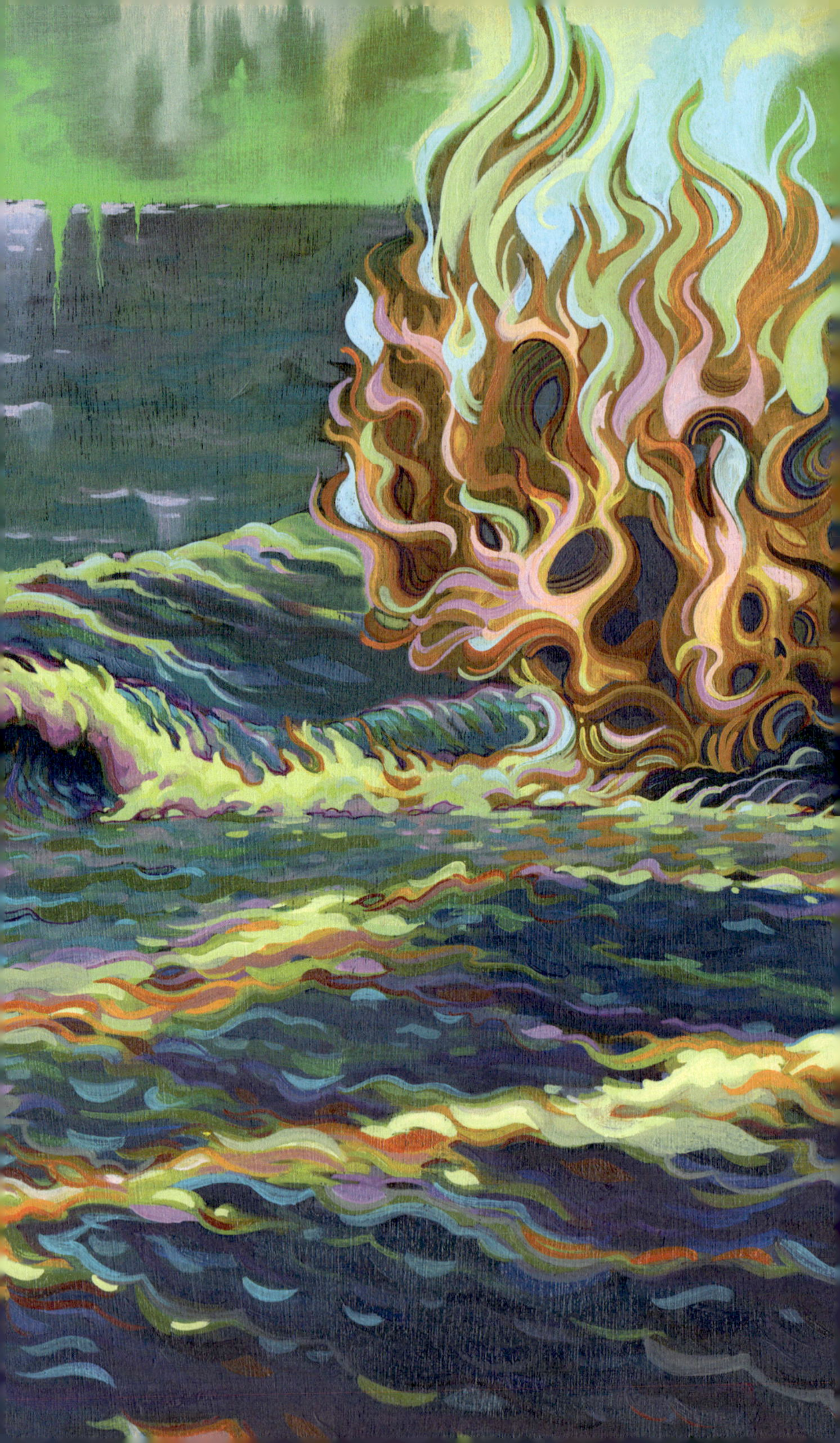

THE 15%

85 percent—the sudden campfire in my nose borne of unnatural fact. Scarlet dawn and dusk, the toxic haze creating a new memory of stars. Of white-wine joys and grilled steelhead atop my Port Orford cedar deck under the clear arena of July's Milky Way. Of serene sundowns with thrushes and nighthawks and cameos of cougar. Of the windless New Moon night limbo and its intense silence that will always easily spark my infinity of thought.

Just 15 percent of American infernos occur naturally. Here in southwest Oregon, innocent dry lightning spawned the Chetco Bar Fire in steep wilds 18 miles from my barbecue on July 15, 2017. Exactly six years before an idiot shot at Tannerite exploding rifle targets and spawned the Flat Fire at dusty Oak Flat Campground 30 miles from my barbecue on July 15, 2023. Nearby Agness (pop. "small") town weather gauge that afternoon peaked at 98°F. Humidity 22 percent. Wind gusting 26 mph from the northeast. No rain in two months.

Exploding targets?

Brilliant.

We marvel at the permanence of human stupidity.

Oak Flat is a diamond in the Rogue River-Siskiyou National Forest rough at the conflux of the Illinois and Rogue rivers an hour east of Gold Beach. Swelling toward 26,000 acres, the new blaze maintains creep to torch remote woods and prairies in a zone known lately for megafires, namely the 100,000-acre Silver (lightning, August 30, 1987), the 500,000-acre Biscuit (lightning, July 13, 2002), the 192,000-acre Chetco Bar, and

he 175,000-acre Klondike (lightning, July 15, 2018). The Fla
s occupying/recycling the revegetated burn scars of the Biscui
and the Klondike, zapping hopeful young stands of tanoak, ma
drone, chinquapin, pine, fir, manzanita, and oh-so-holy Por
Orford cedar.

Chamaecyparis lawsoniana here is acutely native—from
Florence, Oregon, to Ferndale, California. Less than 300 miles
The mountains of counties Coos and Curry are home to the
largest and oldest (+/- 350 years) trees. Today's greatest known
specimen—27 miles east of Port Orford itself—is 229 feet tall
and 12 feet wide. Observable are stumps 20 feet wide.

lawsoniana is per Charles Lawson, the botanic Scot who
circa 19th century led the tree into worldwide horticulture. Its
wood is strong, aromatic, and fine-grained. It resists fire, decay
and insect damage. Here at Purpledeneye I have used it to build
gates, fences, furniture, shelves, boardwalks, stairs, decks. The
wealthy use it to build entire homes. The Japanese use it for
shrines and coffins. It is considered to be the American West's
rarest and most valuable softwood—a relatively boutique and
scarce species, uncultivated commercially. Most of its native
range has been usurped by Douglas fir plantations.

In 1923 a potent Asian pathogen (*Phytophthora lateralis*
was found on the roots of some ornamental Port Orford ceda
seedlings at a nursery in Seattle. Slowly *P. lateralis* slipped south
via water (zoospores) and humans (dirt on shoes, tires, logging
equipment, etc.) before ultimately finding the Coos County
mother lode in 1952. Though not extinctionist, for the tree's
overall survival the disease remains a deep and dire barb.

Fire too. We light 85 percent of them when and where
nature normally will not, extending the West's season from a
historical average of three months to six. Our careless camp
fires, debris piles, machine mishaps, downed power lines, ciga
rettes, arson, gunshots, fireworks, prescribed burns, explodin

targets—unlike summer thunderstorms which often come with rain or light winds and are relatively rare.

Here in most Julys, the aforementions of lightning and stupidity are not rare. Rare is fine surf. Not rare is the finery of Port Orford cedar lumber produced three miles north of Gold Beach and 20 miles southwest of Oak Flat. This is Metcalf Sawmill—snug in the fire's bullseye should it jump the Rogue River and if and when the dry northeasterlies resume.

Recent studies have confirmed that human-caused blazes almost always start in these periods of severe fire weather— hot dry windy antecedent. As with the Flat, there's explosive growth in the first few days, quickly torching thousands of acres and killing nearly four times the number of trees than a slow-moving lightning fire might.

But coastally the wind giveth and the wind taketh. Offshore always swings onshore, scouring quickly the beach skies clean back to glowing blue, the Sun again crystal—the fire a ghost, menacing afar. Like it never happened.

Wave-starved I wheel north for 30 miles along damp unburnable Sitka cliffs which descend to flaxen grass and buildings and the estuary burg of Gold Beach. The Rogue's mouth is jammed with fishing boats angling for steelhead and chinook salmon.

The south jetty—no surf but virgin blue windbrushed conditions. Seals and pelicans bob near shore. North jetty—small surf but chopped and shapeless. I drive on.

Two-lane Highway 101 separates Metcalf's from a strip of forest and a hidden whitesand eden not known for its waves. I peer through the blufftop boughs. Barley Beach—Otter Point— also small, chopped, shapeless. No surfing today.

Unfortunately the wee seaside mill is closed. A visit there is aromatherapy—to be enveloped by Port Orford cedar logs and sawdust—a blessing.

A blessing for us too that some of the biggest trees—mostly dead via *P. lateralis*—remain vertical. Recall the Shrader Old-Growth Grove. Five years since I'd last walked it. Thoroughly magical ancient island 1,200 feet up in the Rogue River-Siskiyou National Forest 13 miles northeast of Gold Beach and a few miles south of the Rogue en route to Agness and Oak Flat. Like Metcalf's—straight down from the fire should it really flare again. Its "incident base" along Jerry's Flat Road is nearly a mile's (and multimillion$') worth of firefighting assets and personnel—a pop-up emergency response village of impressive complexity that looked apocalyptic in the smokeless Sunday shine.

After piercing national forest I weave up into the riverside hills to find the trailhead carpark empty. The path is a fragrant and instant mindwarp into layers of deep time—I'd forgotten the sheer enormity of its firs, alders, and tanoaks, but in the years since my last visit the peculiar sad defeat of the old cedars had haunted me. Bark scars from flames of yore—likely lightning-caused—and, as with redwoods, the trees' thick sponginess shielded them from heavy harm. Instead that would come from a microscopic foe in dirt fecundity, fading the cedars' lush green feminine grace to bare black skeletal snags.

Fracturing the arboreal silence, Flat Fire specters speak through the urgent gnawing whir of helis whizzing upriver. Two miles east of me, the forest is "closed" to public pupils and fresh flames are galloping atop Wild Horse Ridge, three miles east of that area closure boundary. Five miles from the pure air nursing my old-growth meditations.

Fortune favors the wind, I reckon, slowing the fire and teasing it backwards, opposite this grove and Gold Beach civilization. But fortune—good or bad—is the wind itself, cyclical, flared by human ignorance, eased by the impulse of nature.

Modern human nature—slowly flaming out—is estranged from nature nearly 100 percent of the time.

Exploding targets?
Brilliant.
Look at these huge dead Port Orford cedars.
Ask yourself: What is nature 15 percent of the time?

Sunup

Sundown

Flat Fire and the Rogue River.
Photo: Dana Leavitt

Flat Fire.
Photo: US Forest Service

Port Orford cedars and Matt Metcalf of Metcalf Sawmill near Gold Beach.

Rogue River estuary, Gold Beach

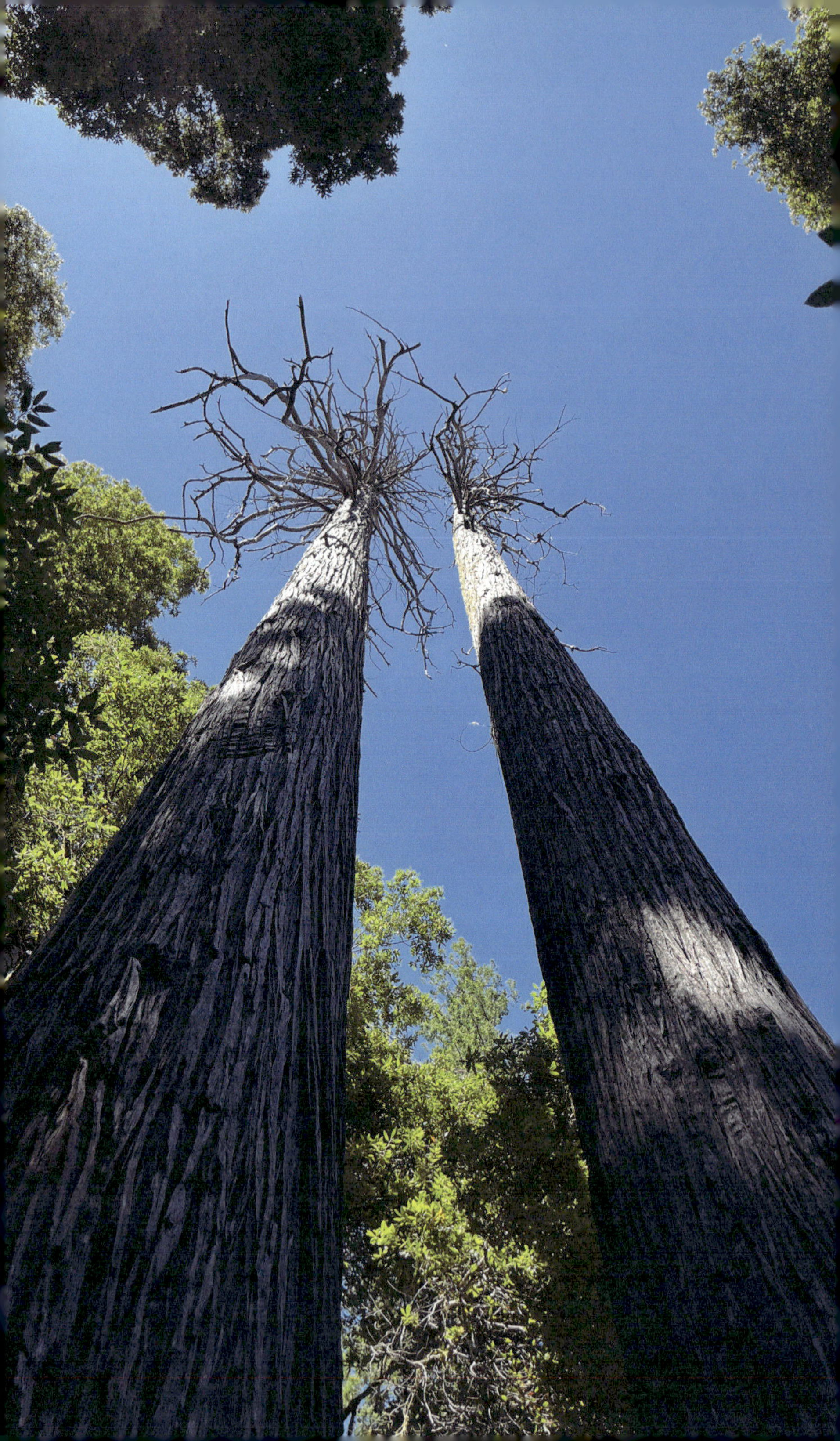

Port Orford cedar

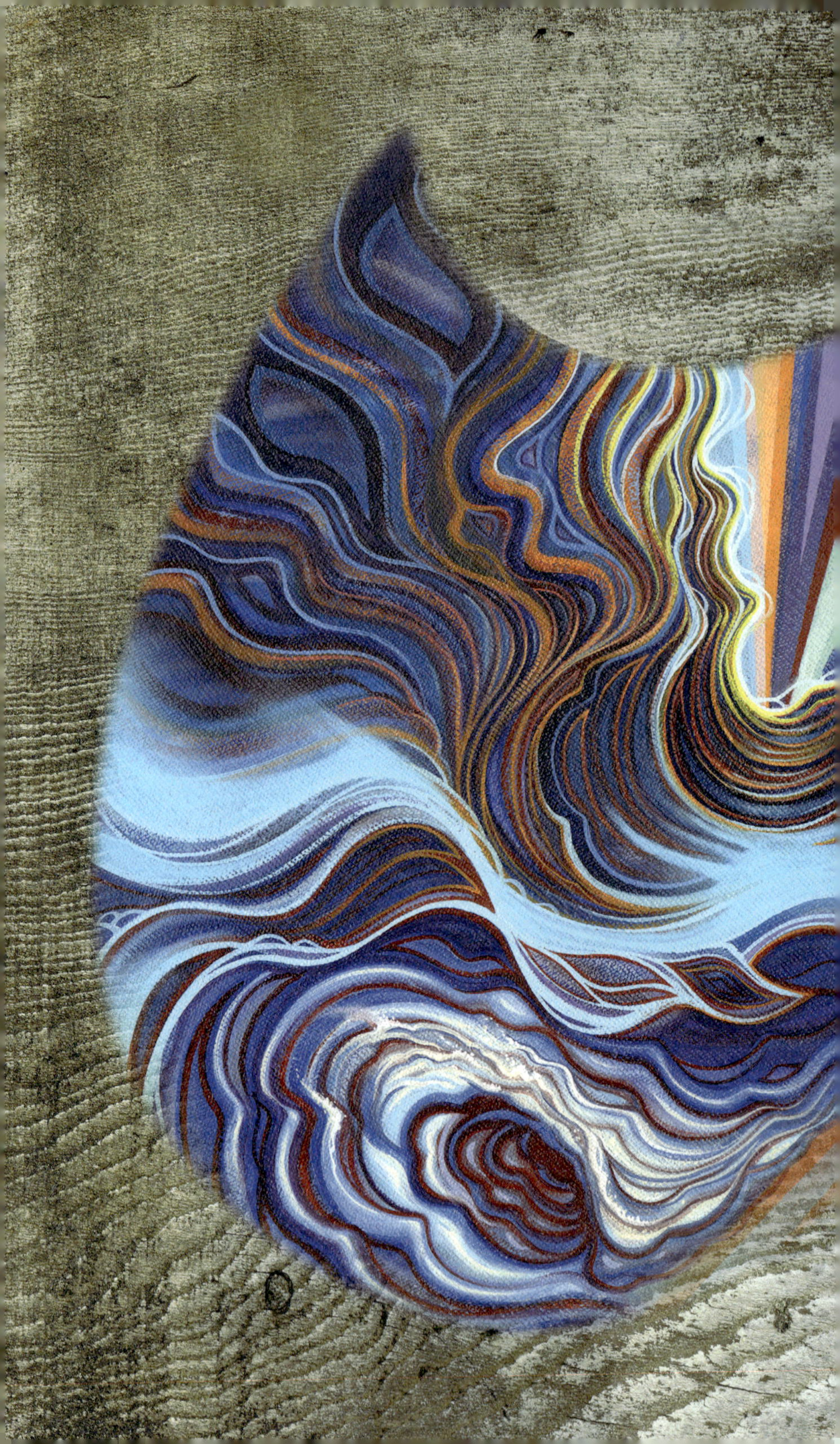

BLUE MOONITY

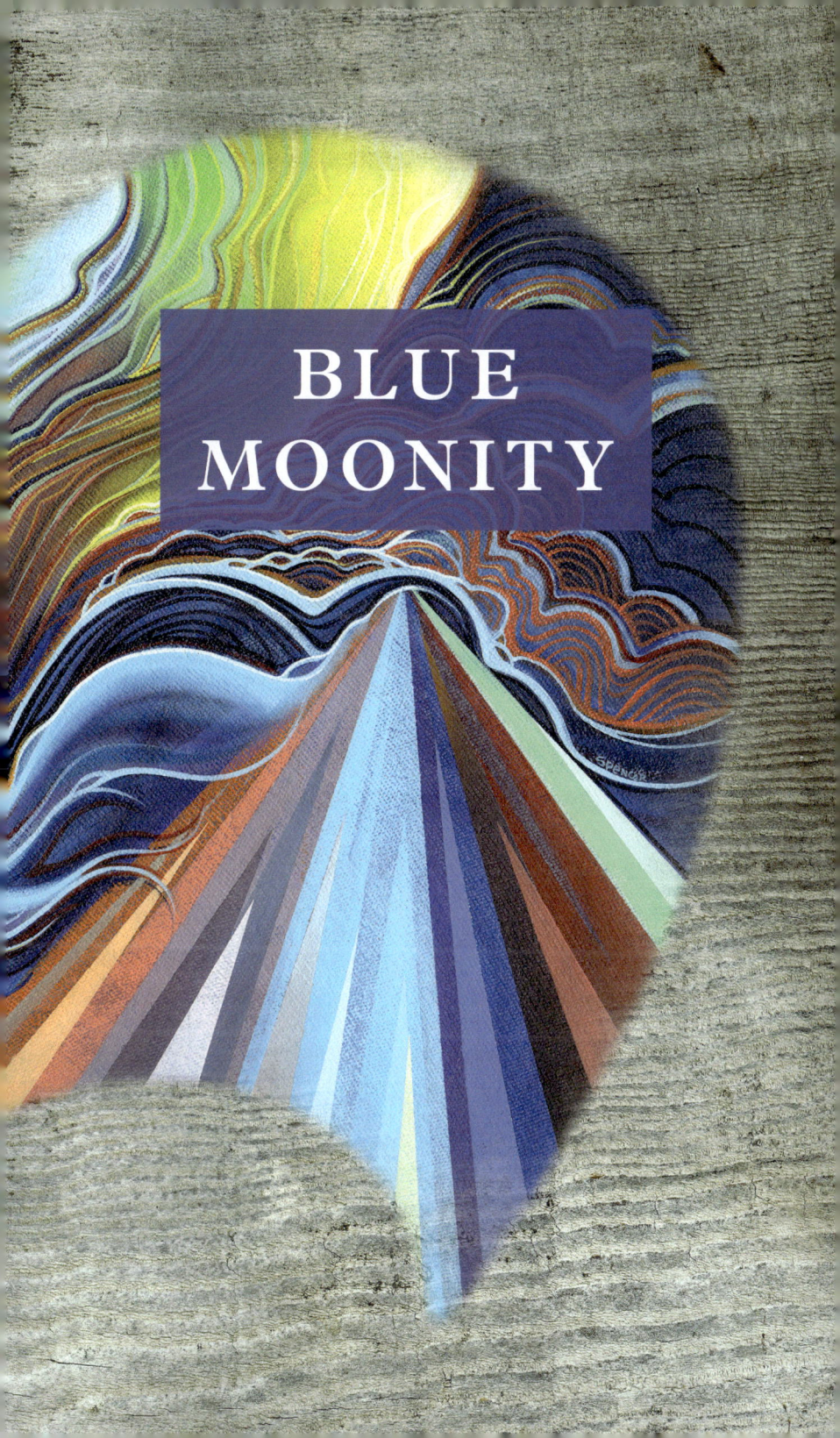

Elevation is separation. Closer to convection. Farther from relaxation.

 Smoke is a force.

 In new drought we dwell.

 Herein the soothing annual return of midsummer night cicadas and crickets and katydids as they tweak and trill like a rust-stuck fire alarm. Lots of those lately. Sirens and Red Flag Warnings. Mountains hushed by smoke. The sad irony of ash in my rain gauge. The thunderstormed omens of August, my 48th birthday month and favorite of the year, sometimes a ragged Leo web of life and death in a creative swirling orientation. Movements include south to San Diego, north to Banff. Lazy river days. Light and shadow. Love and anxiety—abundant like the dry fuels here tempting the sky.

 Spiritual guidance of nature speaks through silent screams of late-night lightning, now frightening. The cloak of unstable encircling air is mythic ether and a wilderness that is a perfect future unto itself but unknowable for anyone until the local flood of flames prompts more toxic oxygen, more evacuations (inland Del Norte County), more road closures (U.S. Highway 199), and more untenable scorched earths (Smith River Complex et al).

 All close yet so far from this faintly glowing Chetco watershed.

 Set down your drink and watch the Moon wax blue.

 Sound familiar?

A "seasonal" Blue Moon as this month's is the third of four full Moons that shall shine within a season—solstice to equinox. Our last such Blue occurred two years yore. Alternatively, August 30 hosts a "monthly" Blue—the second of two full Moons in one month. (In the past decade, just six of the 121 full Moons were blue.) Not only is this the third of four successive supermoons in 2023, it is the closest (222,043 miles out!) and hence the year's largest.

Blue supermoons are rare, yes.

Not as rare as the Moon actually looking blue.

Recall humanity's ancient idiom "the Moon is blue" which had widely referred to any kind of impossibility. This was before 1883 when Krakatoa blew its top. The Indonesian volcano so clogged the atmosphere (nearly 5 cubic miles of rock fragments and a dense mess of ash across 300,000 square miles) that for a while sunsets worldwide were red and the Moon actually did appear blue. The ash particles—each one a micron (one-millionth of a meter) wide—fused with light that bounced off the Moon, scattering the long-wavelengths of red just enough for the bluer hues to spear down into our earthly eyeballs.

This has happened several times in recorded history.

This has also happened during large wildfires.

Lo, "once in a blue moon" blooms as colloquial referent to something occurring rarely, not full-stop-impossibly.

Thunder—happening now. You wait for the ominous flash. Sparse rain, fat drops. Gusty wind. Your nose is piqued for nearby ignitions. There's a new fire up the Winchuck River. Four in the wilds just east of Port Orford. Oblivious orthopteran insects continue to ring deep and true in fractured orange starlight that washes the meadows and parched prairies. Come morning, ocean fogfingers will reach up 'twixt gaps in coastal ridges beneath the hard stinking browns of haze aloft. In southwest Oregon and northwest California, August's lightning will strike not twice not hundreds but thousands of times.

The 2023 Super Blue Moon will receive none. No atmosphere up there. Our beloved celestial body above the holiness of electrostatic discharge. The gravity of our world. Above the smoke and the drought. Up there, yes—above everything. For now. So look down. Sometimes, where would you rather be?

Highway 199.
Photo: Bill Steven

Lone Ranch Beach. Photo: Chris Sackett

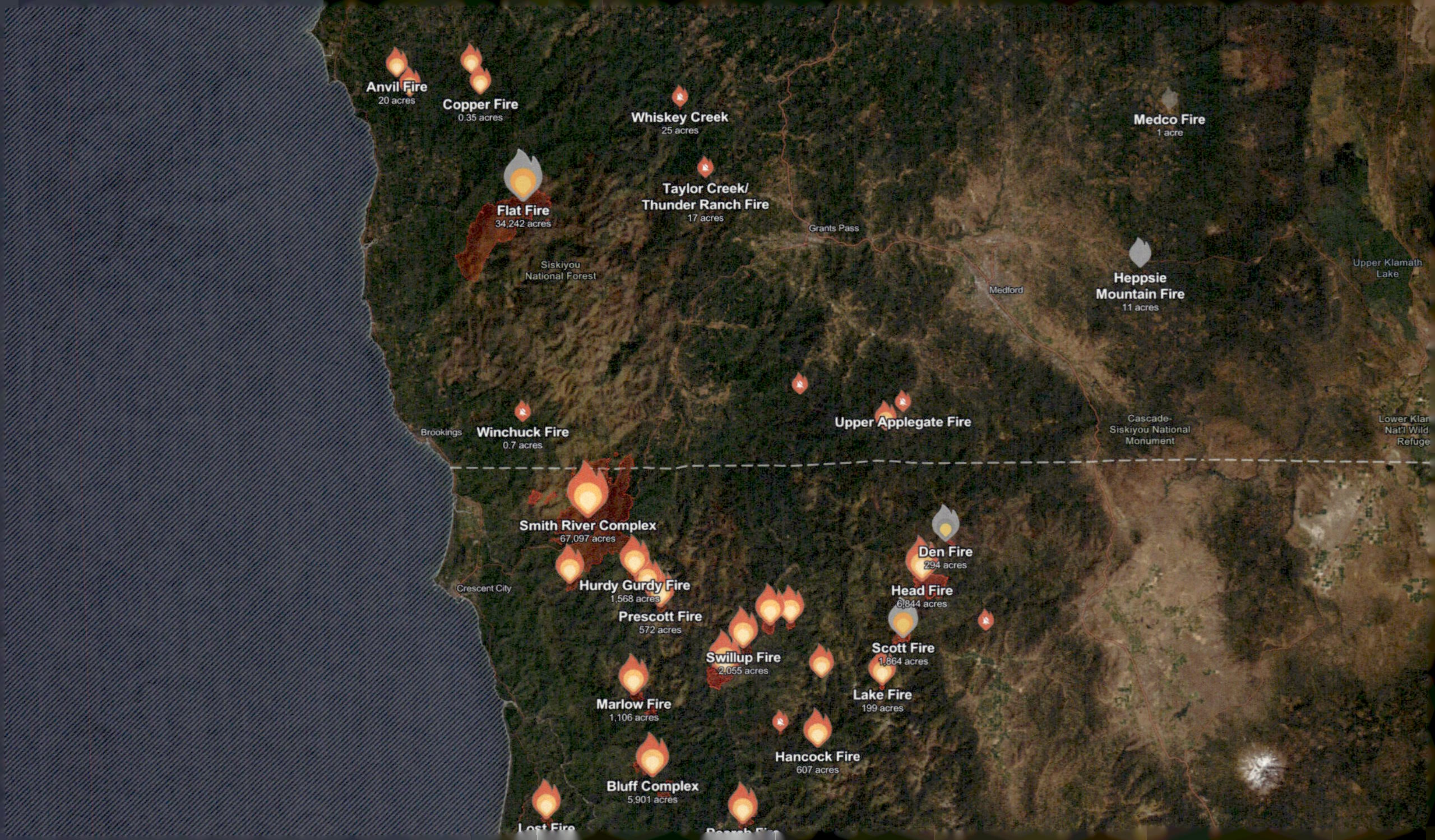

Anvil Fire
20 acres
Copper Fire
0.35 acres
Whiskey Creek
25 acres
Medco Fire
1 acre
Flat Fire
34,242 acres
Taylor Creek/
Thunder Ranch Fire
17 acres
Grants Pass
Siskiyou
National Forest
Medford
Heppsie
Mountain Fire
11 acres
Upper Klamath
Lake
Brookings
Winchuck Fire
0.7 acres
Upper Applegate Fire
Cascade-
Siskiyou National
Monument
Smith River Complex
67,097 acres
Den Fire
294 acres
Head Fire
6,844 acres
Crescent City
Hurdy Gurdy Fire
1,568 acres
Prescott Fire
572 acres
Swillup Fire
2,055 acres
Scott Fire
1,864 acres
Lake Fire
199 acres
Marlow Fire
1,106 acres
Hancock Fire
607 acres
Bluff Complex
5,901 acres

Photo: Space.com

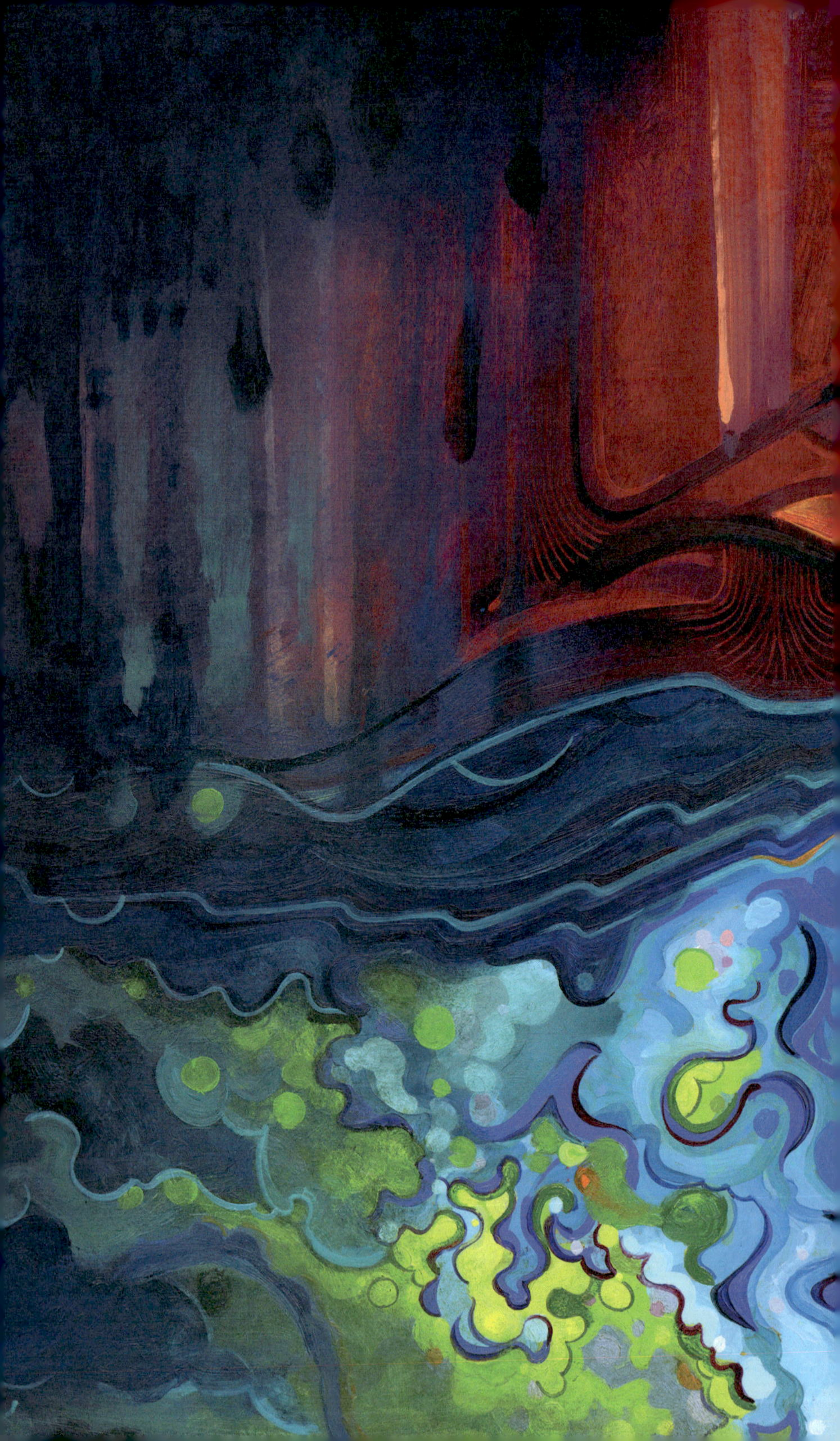

CRIMSON QUEST

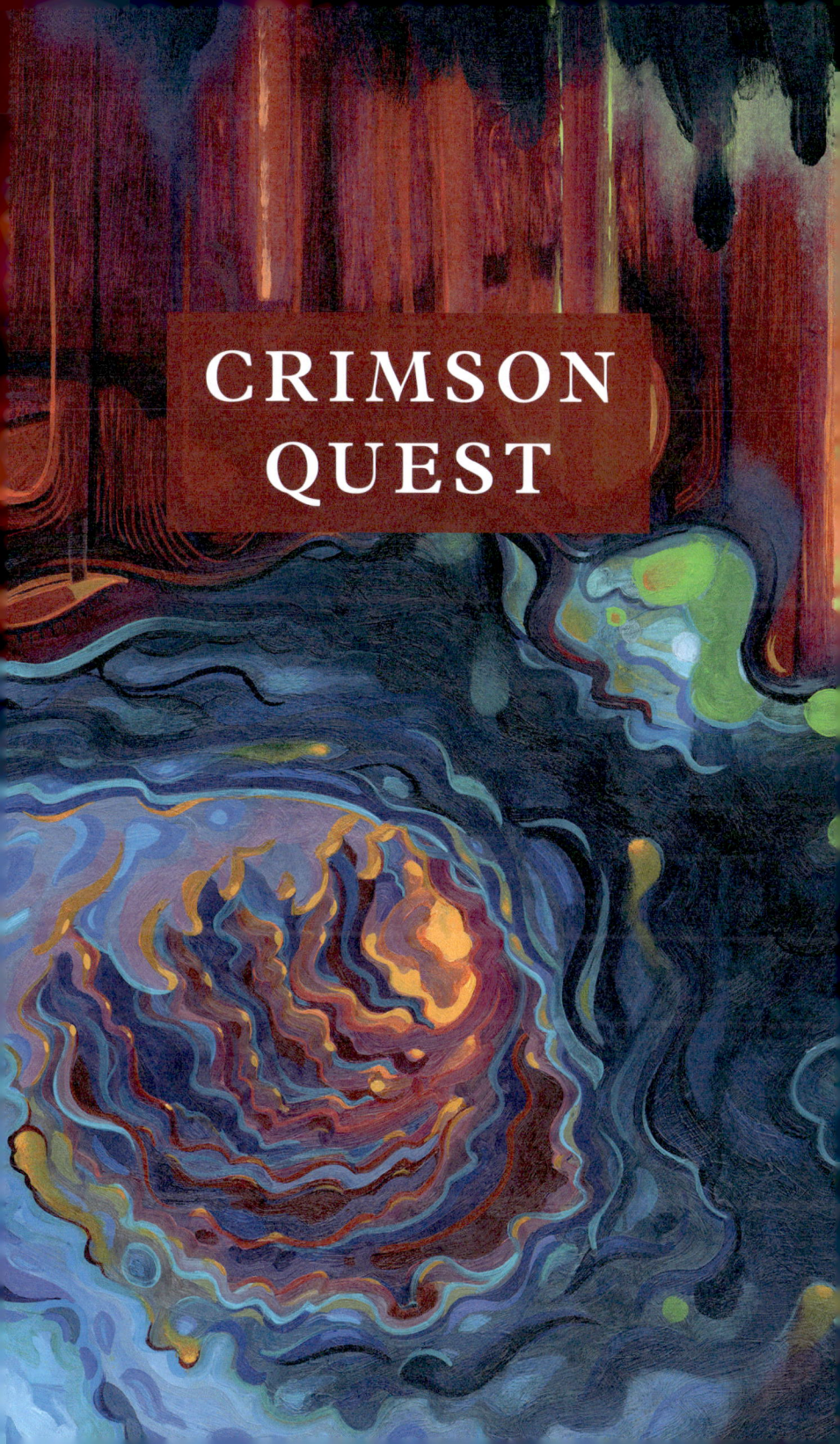

Narrow coastband from Port Orford south through Big Sur—Earth's tallest living things once bristled from two million of these holy acres.

In the 1850s gold was gotten—hives of white humans swarmed west to quadruple Alta California's population. Mining exploded, sawmills sprouted, antique redwoods (*Sequoia sempervirens*) were slaughtered. Today 95 percent—ascending nearly 400 feet and living for more than 2,500 years—are gone.

The five percent? Seventy-seven percent of *those* remain saw-prone on private land. The rest comprise famous parks in central and northern Cal.

"Redwoods, once seen, leave a mark that stays with you," Steinbeck wrote in 1962's *Travels with Charley*. "They are ambassadors from another time."

October 2009. *National Geographic* magazine publishes Joel Bourne's "The Super Trees" immortalizing events of the Redwood Transect, a 1,800-mile south-to-north slog through the scraps of these historic conifers. The transectors—Lindsey Holm and Mike Fay—firstly grokked the southernmost "scattered holdings" in Monterey County. Eleven months on, the two had searched and slogged through deep brush six or so miles north of the state line.

I paused and smiled near the story's end: "On the last day of their transect, as they hunted for the northernmost redwood near Oregon's Chetco River. . . . "

Here, having somewhat avoided sawteeth, a handful of ancients dot the watershed. And in the Rogue River-Siskiyou

National Forest, with their road signage, toilets, picnic tables, and self-guided interpretive brochures, two small groves are easily reached.

After reading the *National Geographic* story and growing evermore curious per coordinates of our absolute northernmost naturally occurring redwood tree, I studied a big Forest Service map of my locality. One obscure triangle of land: 21-acre Snaketooth Redwood Botanical Area. Below this were Big and Little Redwood creeks, drooling into the Chetco's south bank.

In March 2018 Klamath Forest Alliance's Luke Ruediger sent a blog entry detailing his Quail Prairie Creek canyon inspection per its proposed post-Chetco Bar Fire salvage logging, an evil dream of the Forest Service. Recalling the *National Geographic* line, I was piqued: "In a few locations young redwoods can be found growing among forests once dominated by Douglas fir. In one location we found . . . a single redwood tree, scorched by the fire, but responding with vigorous, green basal sprouts throughout the trunk. This tree, likely spread into the area from the nearby Snaketooth Butte redwood stands, is located within a roadside hazard unit. The entire stand . . . will be removed in the roadside logging prescriptions . . . (and) will potentially damage the isolated redwood, reducing its viability."

I placed Quail Prairie Creek at more than six miles north of the aforementioned redwood sites and 10 miles north of Oregon's most famous redwoods that are literally downmountain from my house.

Wheeling for one minute past Alfred A. Loeb State Park (should be indigenously renamed Chetco State Park), where the air speaks of moss and camphor, motorists will find a small dirt carpark fronting a rectangular isle of old-growth forest amid myriad clearcuts and commercial fir plantations.

Looping through this 50-acre prize, Redwood Nature Trail is a popular 1.1-mile walk. The path snakes up and down a slope bisected by Two Salmon Creek and other seasonal streams gurgling to the Chetco. Sun-dappled canopies and lush understories here show us how the areal non-prairied hills once looked, smelled, and vibed.

In August 2017 the Chetco Bar Fire nearly nixed everything but via firefighting efforts the grove was narrowly saved. Not so lucky were the Wheeler Creek Research Natural Area (prime old-growth redwoods), Redwood Bar Campground, and the Snaketooth Redwood Botanical Area. Most of the affected trees, however, with their thick fire-resistant bark, endured scant damage. High in tannins, redwood bark has no resin nor pitch and hence burns slowly.

The trail's biggest redwoods are anywhere from three to eight centuries old and live at the top of the loop. The northernmost 300-footer is found here. Unique in that the largest are normally at lower, flatter elevations.

"I suspect it has to do with cold air sinking into the canyons in winter and potentially causing tree tops to freeze. But I'm not sure. The Chetco is a special place as it is not only one of the coldest valleys where redwoods grow but also one of the warmest. It has the greatest temperature variation of anywhere redwoods live besides maybe Napa County."

This was Zane Moore, jovial chap and scholar of redwood genomes at University of California, Davis. In April 2022 *National Geographic* published another redwoods article wherein writer Nadia Drake explored the tree's albino oddities. ("A biological improbability—an organism that shouldn't exist . . . a scientific puzzle.") Moore was the story's protagonist.

I wondered if he'd found any albinos near Brookings.

"The northernmost known specimen is in California's Jedediah Smith Redwoods State Park," he said. "I would *love* to know about any albino redwoods you find up there, though. Keep your eye out for big yellow branches in the trees."

Fourteen miles north of Jedediah Smith (should be renamed Tolowa Dee-ni' Redwoods State Park per the region's indigenous tribe) lies the also-lamely-named Oregon Redwoods Trail. This land—from Peavine Ridge east a few miles to Bear Ridge—is home to Oregon's largest *Sequoia sempervirens*.

". . . . including a 322-foot-tall one and a 22-foot-wide diameter one," Moore said. "The largest is a bit over 22,000 cubic feet, about half the size of the largest redwoods in Jedediah Smith. But these trees are not easily accessible. They're a decent bushwhack in the Peavine area. Are you able to do that? Would you like to go see them?"

Thirty-five years ago, Oregon Redwoods Trail was almost another clearcut. On Peavine Ridge, around the top of the Moser Creek drainage, the Forest Service sought to log 60 acres of public land for a quick three million board feet. Thankfully the old trees were saved and can forever be enjoyed by all—even loggers.

One September yore, just past the equinox and beneath a Harvest Moon shrouded in blue, via mountain bike and foot I'd poked around Quail Prairie Creek for what's likely the world's northernmost naturally occurring coast redwood. Miles off the mark, Fay and Holm didn't find it. Neither have I—yet.

Thirst and hunger and dark Mozart sonatas rode me back to my car and civilization for a burger and French fries.

Slouched on his mobility scooter at the next table coincidentally was a thin beatific man—an ex-logger, perhaps 80—sipping coffee and reading a newspaper. He glanced over and asked why my clothes were splattered with mud.

"Yeah, we used to pull a *lot* of big redwood outta there," he said, gargle-voiced. "Not many of 'em left—is that right?"

Those fries—much too salty.

Two Salmon Creek

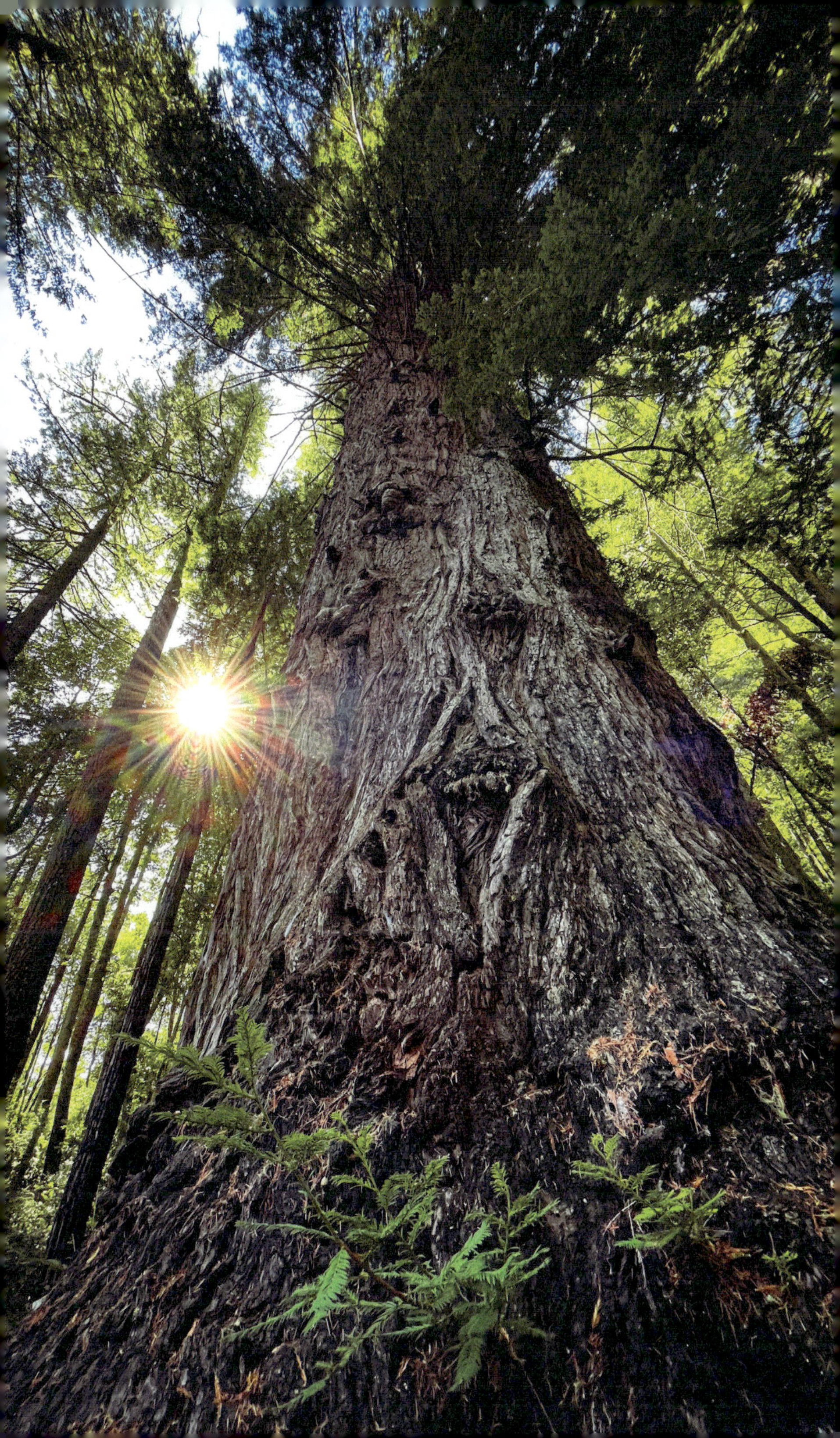

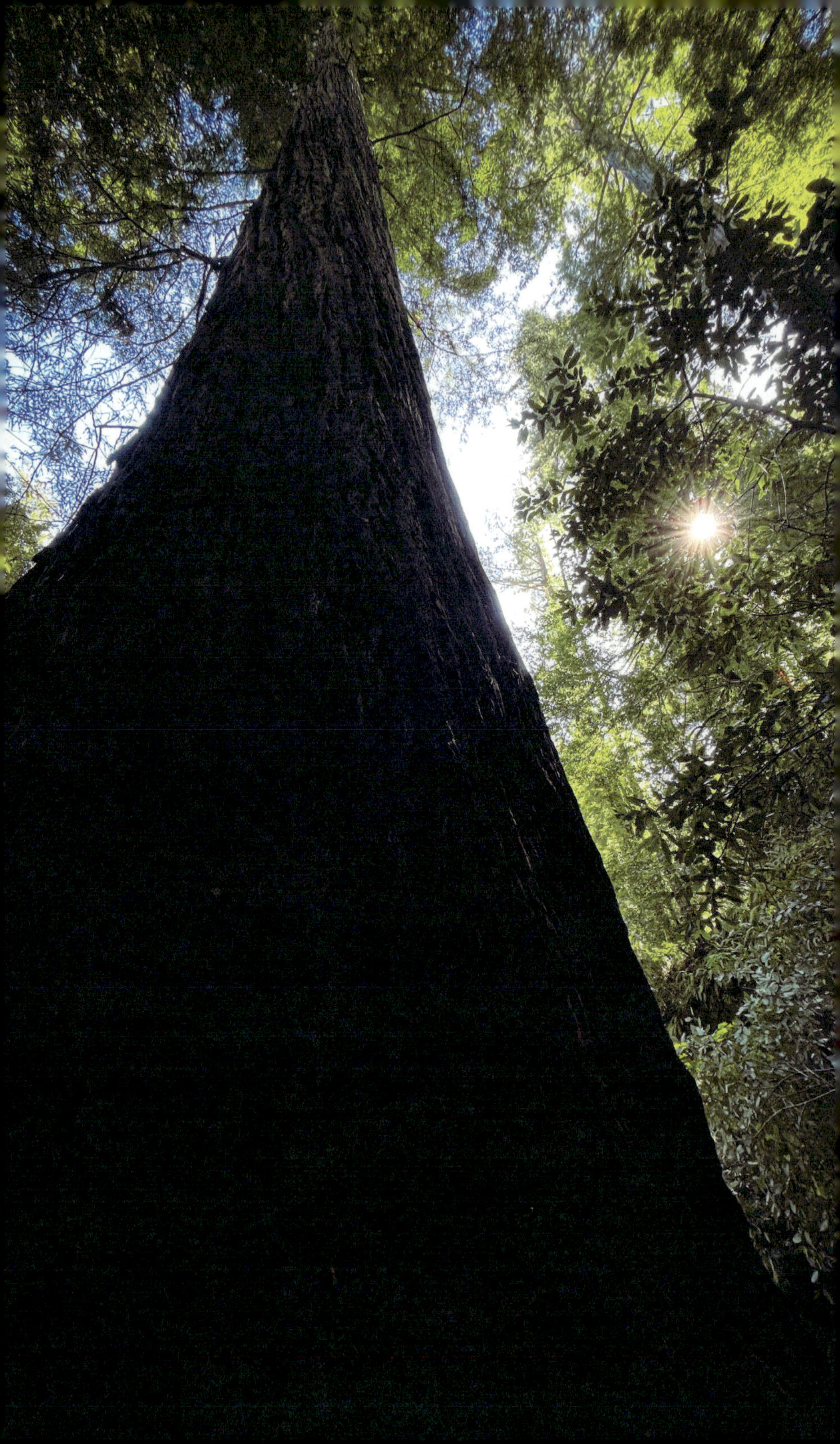

Photo courtesy Curry Historical Society

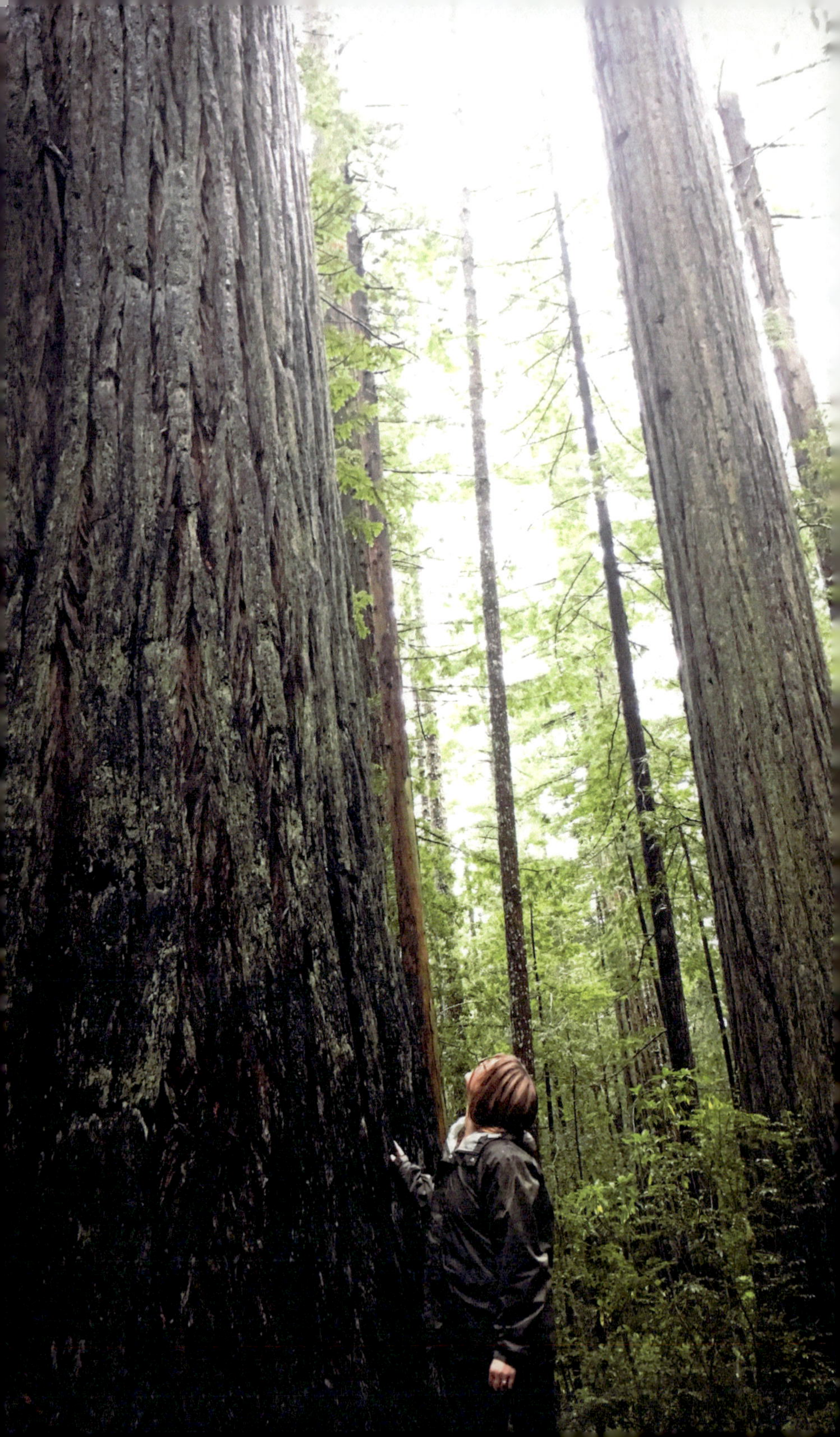

Coast redwood

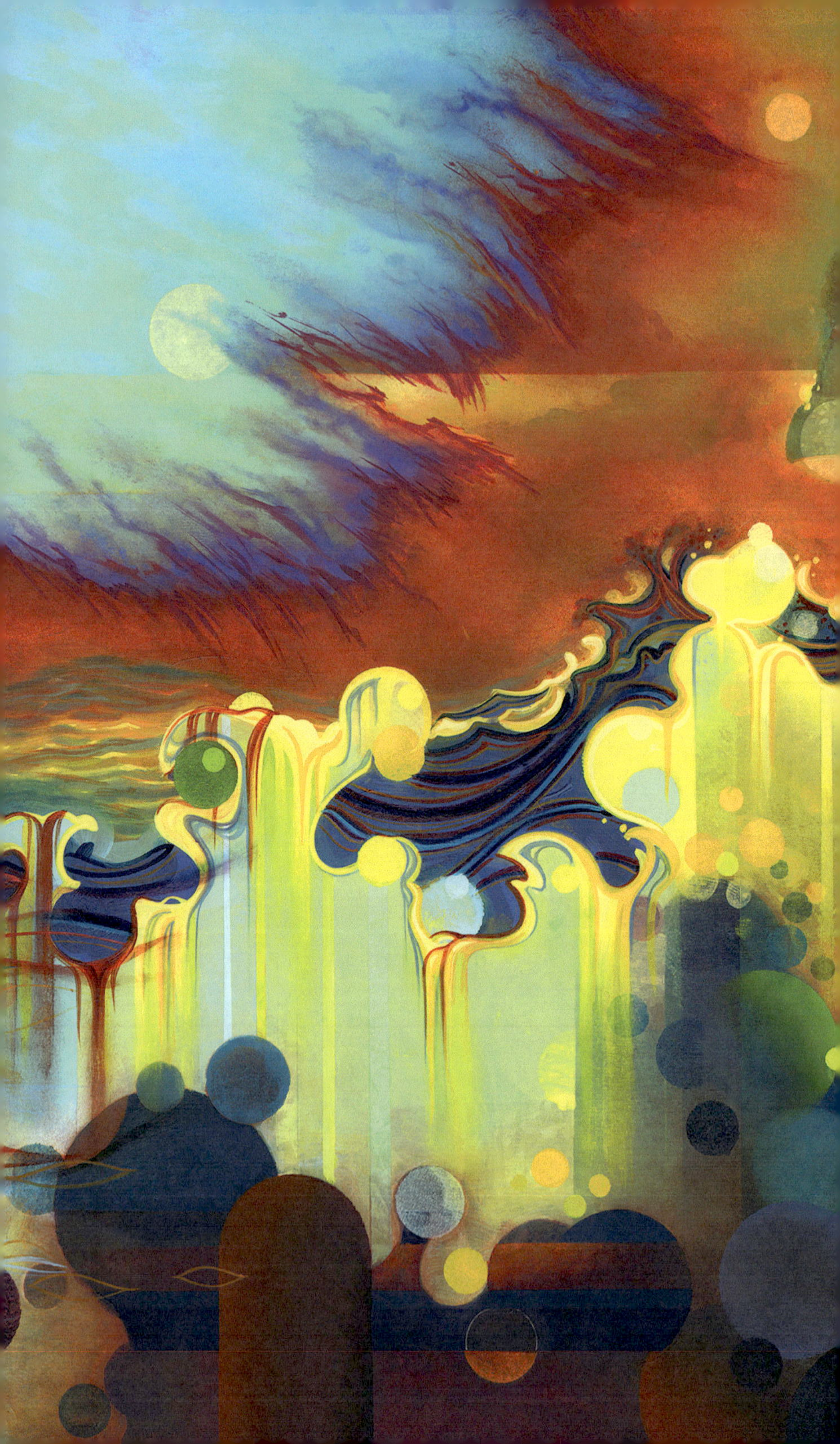

OCTOBER IN THE HALOED EARTH*

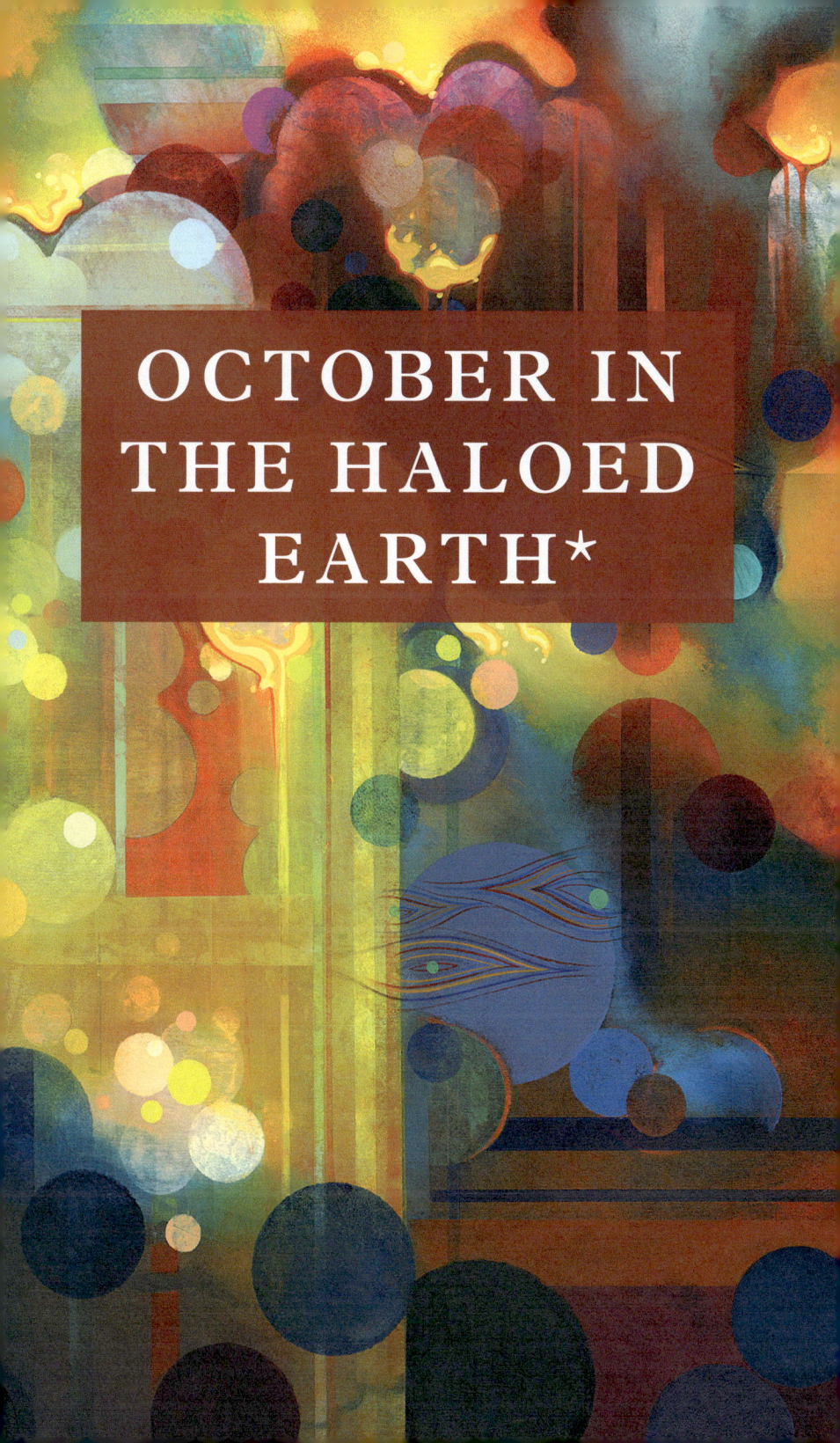

A blessing: heat hum trails the equinoctial rain. River: fishy, algae-freed. Reflexes of myrtle and maple laze upon its jadecrystal waters pulsing like aurora borealis in the hot-hung pause of afternoon.

Quintessence: Indian Summer.

Clear quiet days of reverie and nights of tinkling crickets and creeping bears beneath Saturn and Jupiter and waning crescent Moon would all approach the annularity that coastally was not. Low clouds killed the south Oregon shore. Yet the shadows of soul? They grew.

Apt for October.

It would come eighth (Latin *octo* = "eight") in the 10-month Roman calendar which of course Caesar stretched to 12. Later Octobers finished with Samhain, even later the pagan Iron Age seed of Halloween and the last "festival" in the ancient Celts' eightfold year wheel. This was and is a cosmic spin entailing four based solar—two equinoxes, two solstices—and four based lunar: Imbolc (start of spring), Beltane (start of summer), Lughnasadh (start of harvest), Samhain (end of harvest).

As a late-'80s teen I saw the Gaelic word in the form of an American deathrock/horror punk band led by Glenn Danzig of Misfits fame (both bands boosted my tinnitus). Years on I learned that Samhain, pronounced *sow-wen*, was not merely a mysterious quartet of scowling men but something much larger and older spiritually hinging summer to winter, a liminal (Latin *limen* = "threshold") space whence the veil between physical and spiritual worlds—between us and our ancestors—is thinnest.

Scorpio, the latter a water (autumn rain?)-based astrological sign that rules the eighth of each year's 12 horoscopic "houses." These are found also in the zodiac wheel, a 360-degree chart denoting the 12 signs (mine is Leo).

The houses (spaced 30 degrees apart) follow the yearlong ecliptic plane through which the Sun travels. Each house is paired with a constellation (zodiac sign) and a planet. Like each sign, each house has unique personality traits, fortunes, futures, and symbolisms.

For you and me, astrologers take these planetary positions and the jive between them to define and cast natal charts—the chart a glimpse of the heavens at the precise time and place we were born. It's a dozen tidy sects, each tied to whichever astrological house and month they fall within. Devised by Babylonians in 1500 BCE, all 12 houses have distinct themes.

Our current zodiacal theme, then, is one of transition and transformation—of sex and death, of beginnings and endings. Even at a microvegetative scale here around Brookings, with the brown summerdead forbs and grasses reborn green after the cyclical early-autumn rains and still-warm sunshine that soothes the still-warm topsoils and freshening the now-chilled watershed. The way the west-wind-driven clouds will blow in from the Pacific to block and filter the ever-sinking beam of Sun and blanket the Earth in fleeting shadow.

Much like an annular eclipse.

Mid-month, for millions of lucky eyes, the Moonblocked Sun fused the illusion of a vertical orange halo, a black hole ringed, a cavity of ringing bells. The light dimmed, the light brightened. The veil between day and night laid bare. On a windy cape, we missed it all. Rain would occur. (Ironically thick wildfire smoke denied me the 2017 total eclipse.)

Life by sundial moves faster than death. So I can still dream and admire the wheel. About the fire of sublimity torquing tha first shift in light as it bows deep into the ancestral yawn. I can doze in damp grass on a Hunter's Moon ridgetop prairie and feel the last bones and footprints of prior lives living forth in these loams and rock forests and subsoil microbial eternities. All beneath ear-ringing limbos of aforementioned tinnitus.

Dazzled by Venus before it drops into the peaks, I can revere the lambent zodiacal light of the Kalmiopsis in a misty skydawn of dawns following that elusive ring of fire. Dawns that will rapidly sink colder and wetter. Dawns for a mind rapidly withdrawing to the orange ataraxic glow found at a woodstove of sap-crackle per the huge Kalmiopsis-facing fir felled last winter by a southern gale.

There's an ambient gap between September and October where you first smell the star-tickling woodsmoke in lengthening night. There's the remembrance of loved ones gone. There's the clang of autumn resembling a dark mountain song, a slow plunge from the warm peak of summer down to the meditation valley of winter. There's the mnemonic Orkney glug of Highland Park whisky poured into my Glencairn glass—something I always do on or near Samhain, when I also exhume my three Samhain albums and play each at least once.

All of this and more—messages from a distant past.

Back amongst myrtles and maples aside the river Chetco. See the ancient king and Chinook salmon, leaping, dodging fishhooks, weaving upstream to spawn. If they can. The slim veil of life and death. Though time gets away, seasonal voices always tell us where we are.

Nod to Kerouac's "October in the Railroad Earth" prose poem, penned in San Francisco, Calif., October 1952.

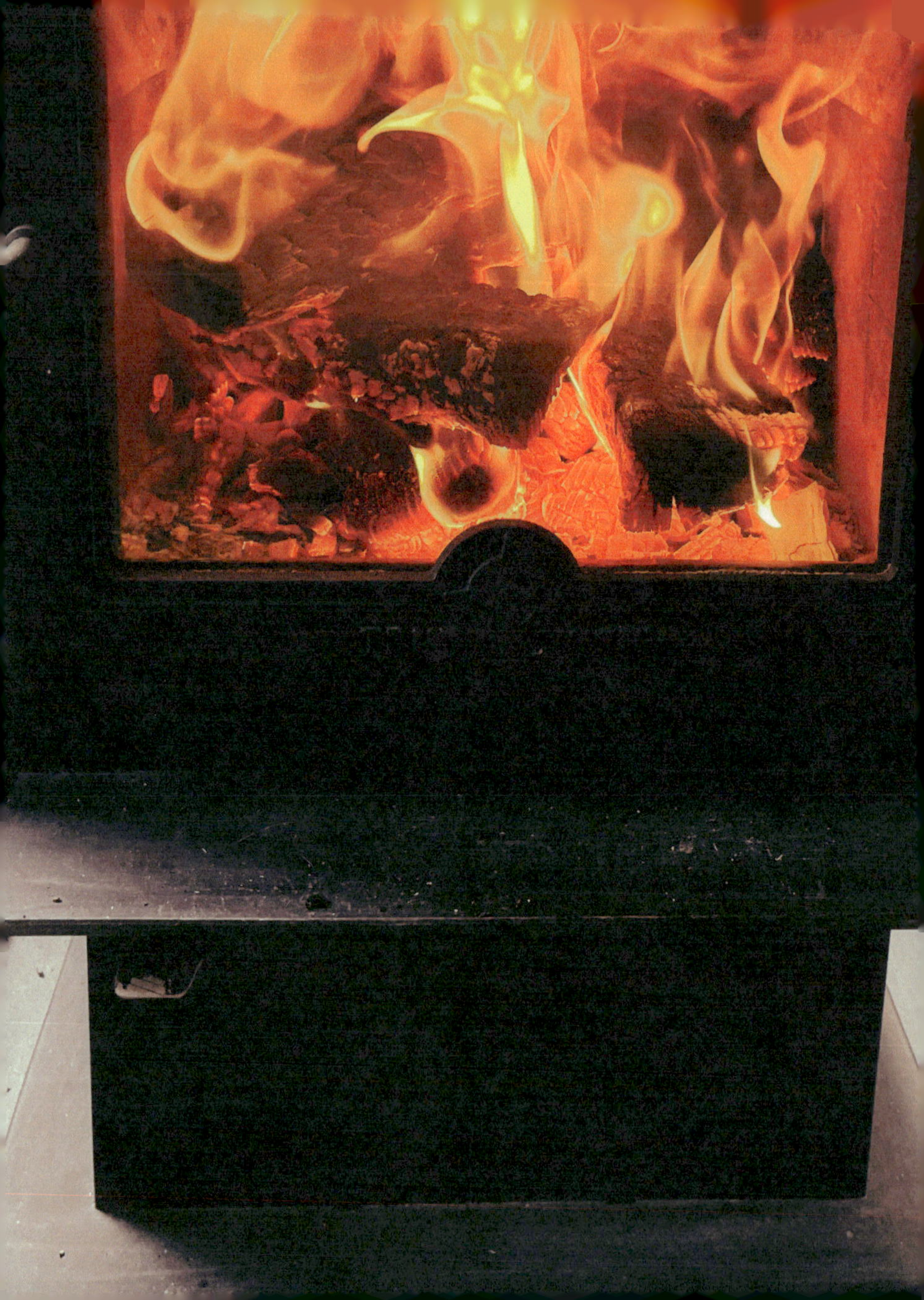

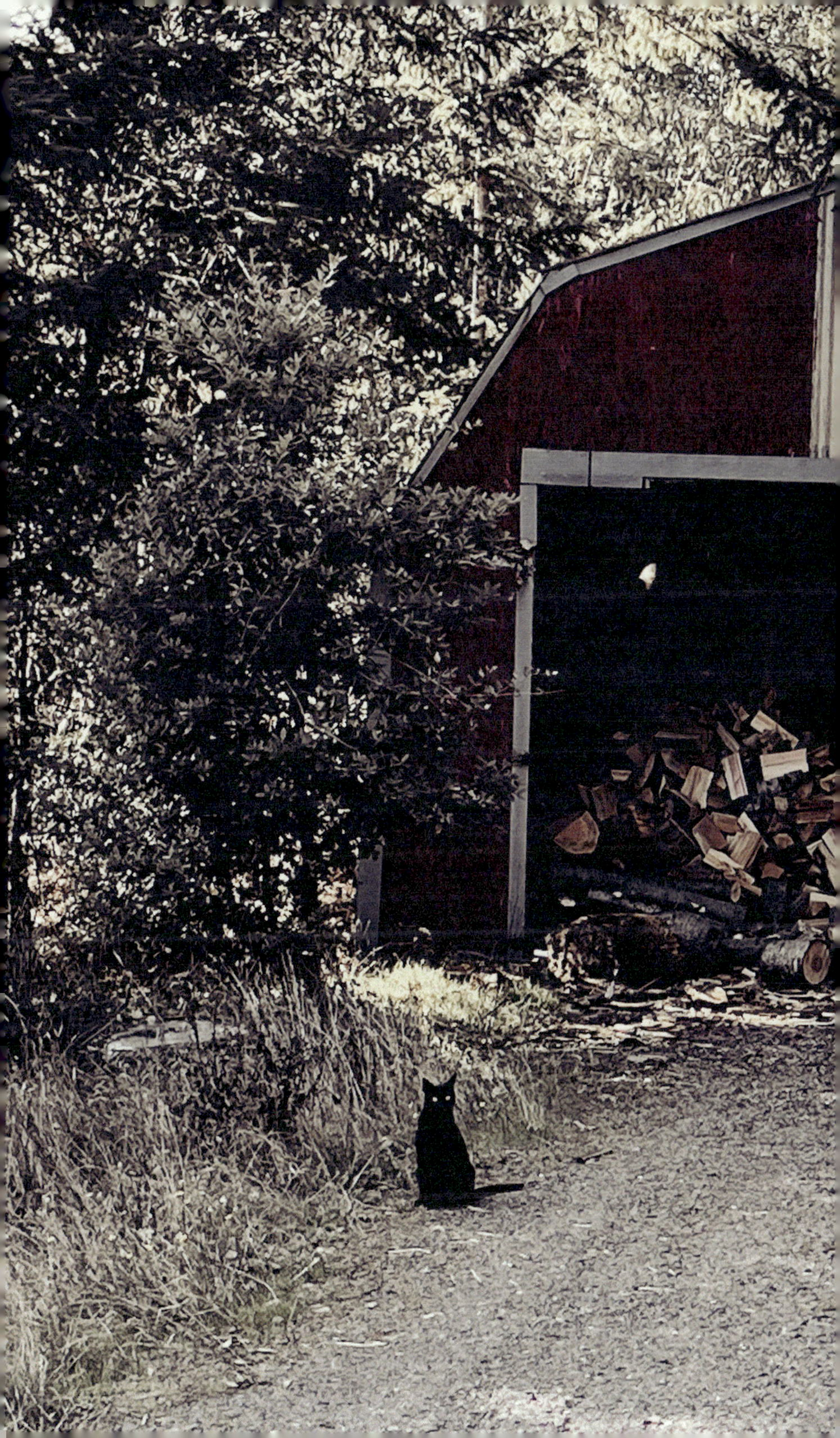

Tolowa Coast

Chetco River

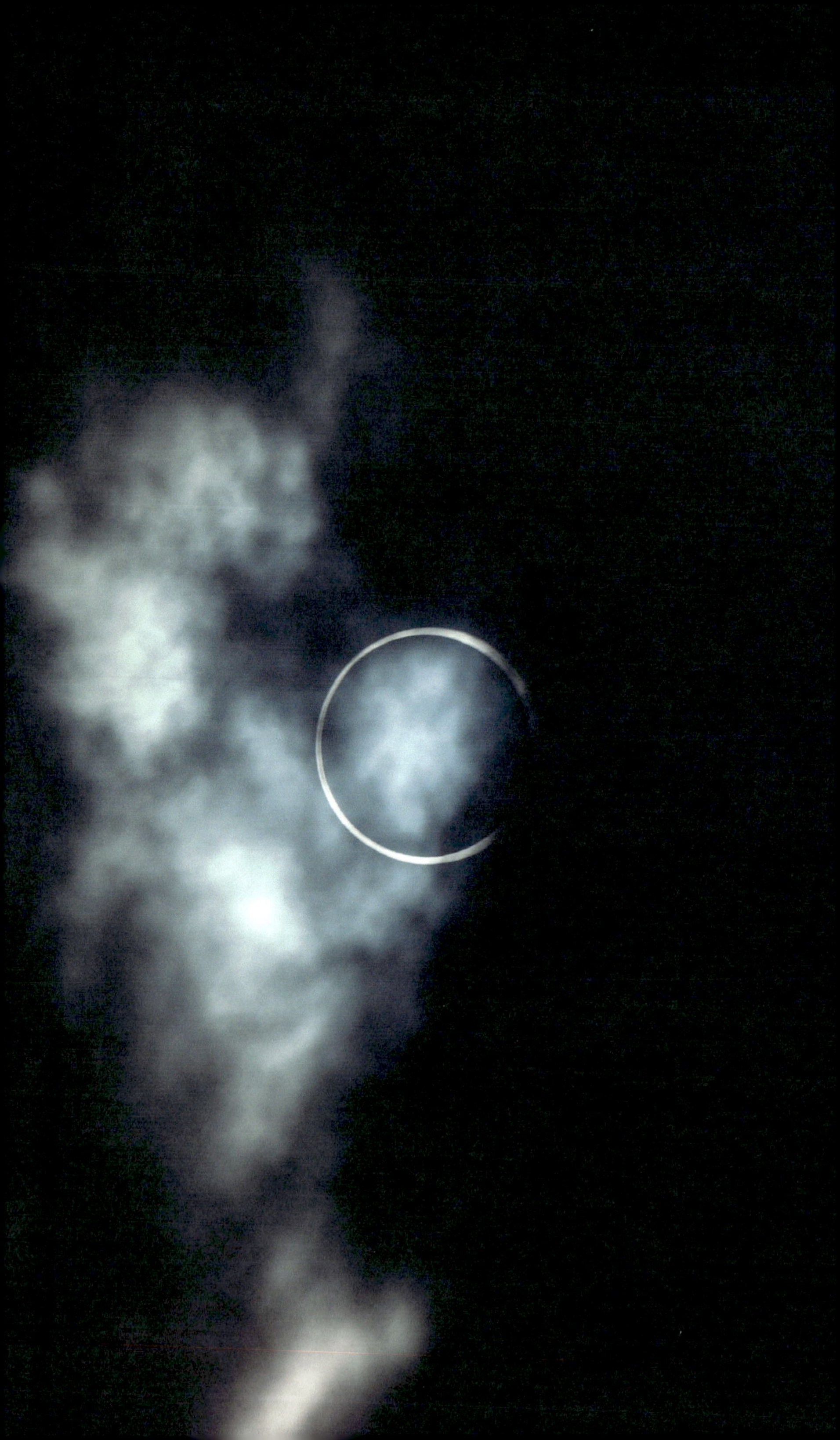

JACK KEROUAC: October in the Railroad Earth

THERE WAS A LITTLE ALLEY IN SAN FRANCISCO back of the Southern Pacific station at Third and Townsend in redbrick of drowsy lazy afternoons with everybody at work in offices in the air you feel the impending rush of their commuter frenzy as soon they'll be charging en masse from Market and Sansome buildings on foot and in buses and all well-dressed thru workingman Frisco of Walkup ?? truck drivers and even the poor grime-bemarked Third Street of lost bums even Negroes so hopeless and long left East and meanings of responsibility and *try* that now all they do is stand there spitting in the broken glass sometimes fifty in one afternoon against one wall at Third and Howard and here's all these Millbrae and San Carlos neat-necktied producers and commuters of America and Steel civilization rushing by with San Francisco *Chronicles* and green *Call-Bulletins* not even enough time to be disdainful, they've got to catch 130, 132, 134, 136 all the way up to 146 till the time of evening supper in homes of the railroad earth when high in the sky the magic stars ride above the following hotshot freight trains—it's all in California, it's all a sea, I swim out of it in afternoons of sun hot meditation in my jeans with head on handkerchief on brakeman's lantern or (if not working) on book, I look up at blue sky of perfect lostpurity and feel the warp of wood of old America beneath me and have insane conversations with Negroes in several-story windows above and everything is pouring in, the switching moves of boxcars in this little alley which is so much like the alleys of Lowell and I hear far off in the sense of coming night that engine calling our mountains.

BUT IT WAS THAT BEAUTIFUL CUT OF CLOUDS I could always see above the little S.P. alley, puffs floating by from Oakland

From Evergreen Review, *vol. 1#2, Grove Press, 1957*

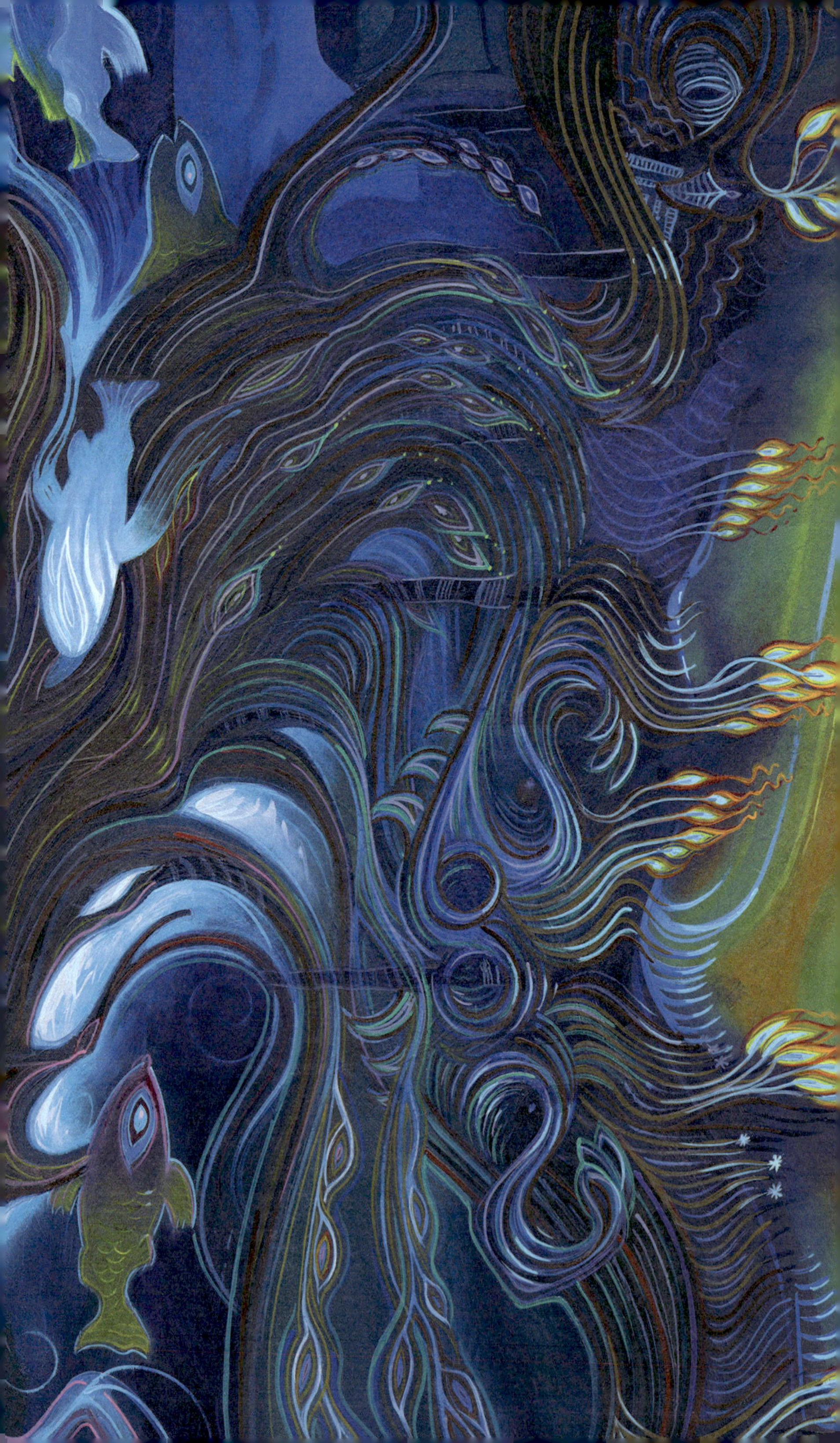

TRINITY
TOPAZ

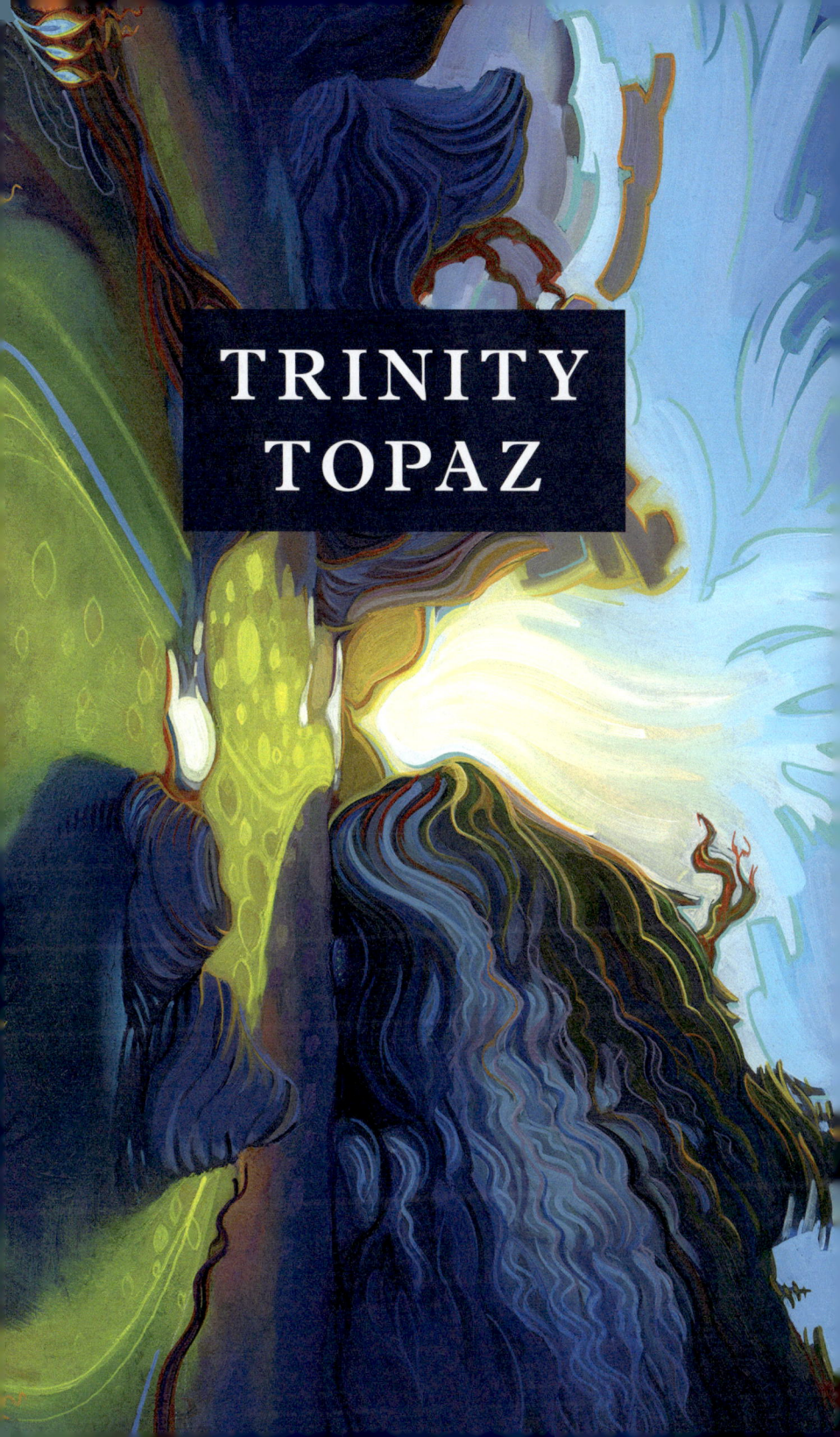

Come—wake with me beneath the liquid hush of mountain prairie where can I find you amongst the chimera of time. Where we can zoom down through the bright leaves of alder and maple, midday winds splashing topaz all across the death of Oregon's autumn.

Topaz—one of November's two birthstones. See that it shines through myriad hues. Feel it cool and hard beneath your soles as we stroll aside the coastal stream. Admire the otter, the osprey, the bat, the bald eagle. The frog and the salamander. Beaver Moon strolls with us too.

Espresso—cold windy morn at the beach. Fine surf. No surfers. Further you saturate my mind. Eyes flood with the yellows of beach grass and large driftwood. The yellows of glare as it blinds my steep take-offs over the shallow sandbar. Yellows of the glitter tickling the rivermouth tissues of chinook salmon. Here they spawn in sanctuaries beneath the bare bones of waterside Winchuck woods tumbling in and out of the Siskiyou wilds.

Yellows—of.

This—nature's entropy. The universe's permanent lock.

Unlock—it.

Sharpen—it. So we can cut through life and flow like river. Whatever forever. Early and late rains will rush in, spliced with Sun and spearing the verdure of our dreaming fields. Solar flares slip ever south daily as winter will whisper its new tales to us. About us. About you and me in this newly soul-churned light.

Light—of yellow love.

Winchuck River

Chinook salmon

Beaver Moon

Atop Chetco Point

Bigleaf maple

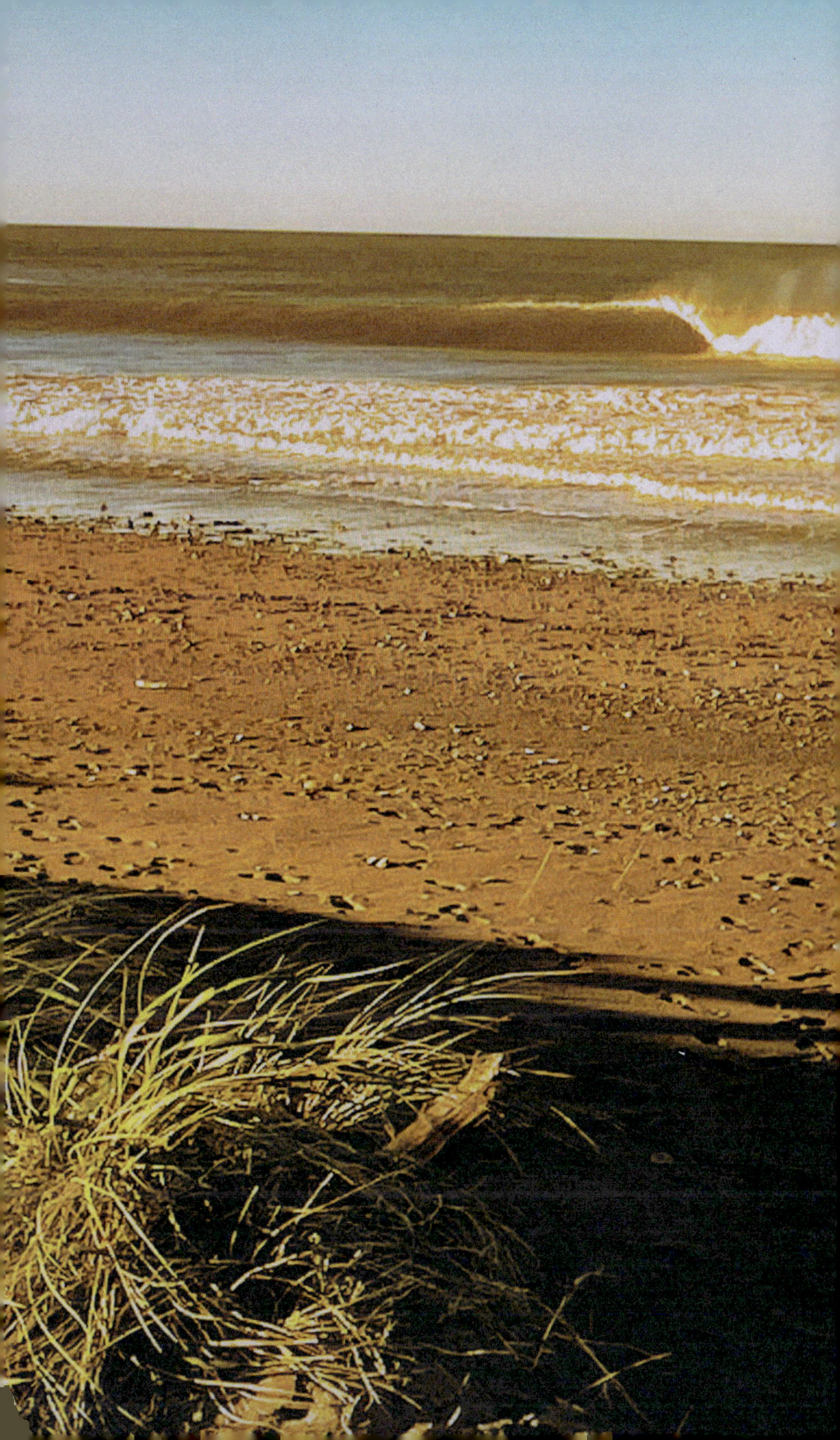

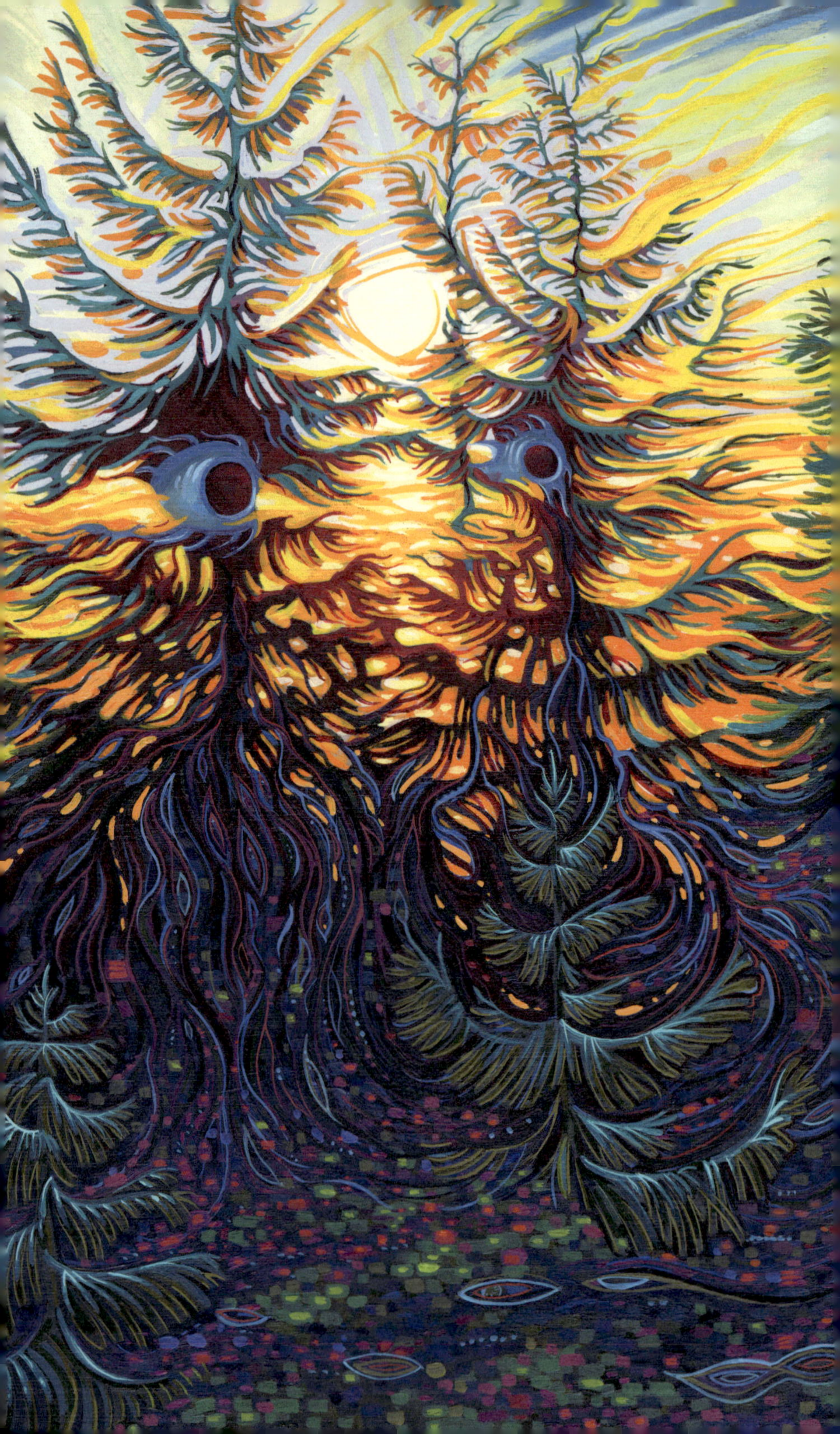

UNDEAD IN THE EVERGREEN

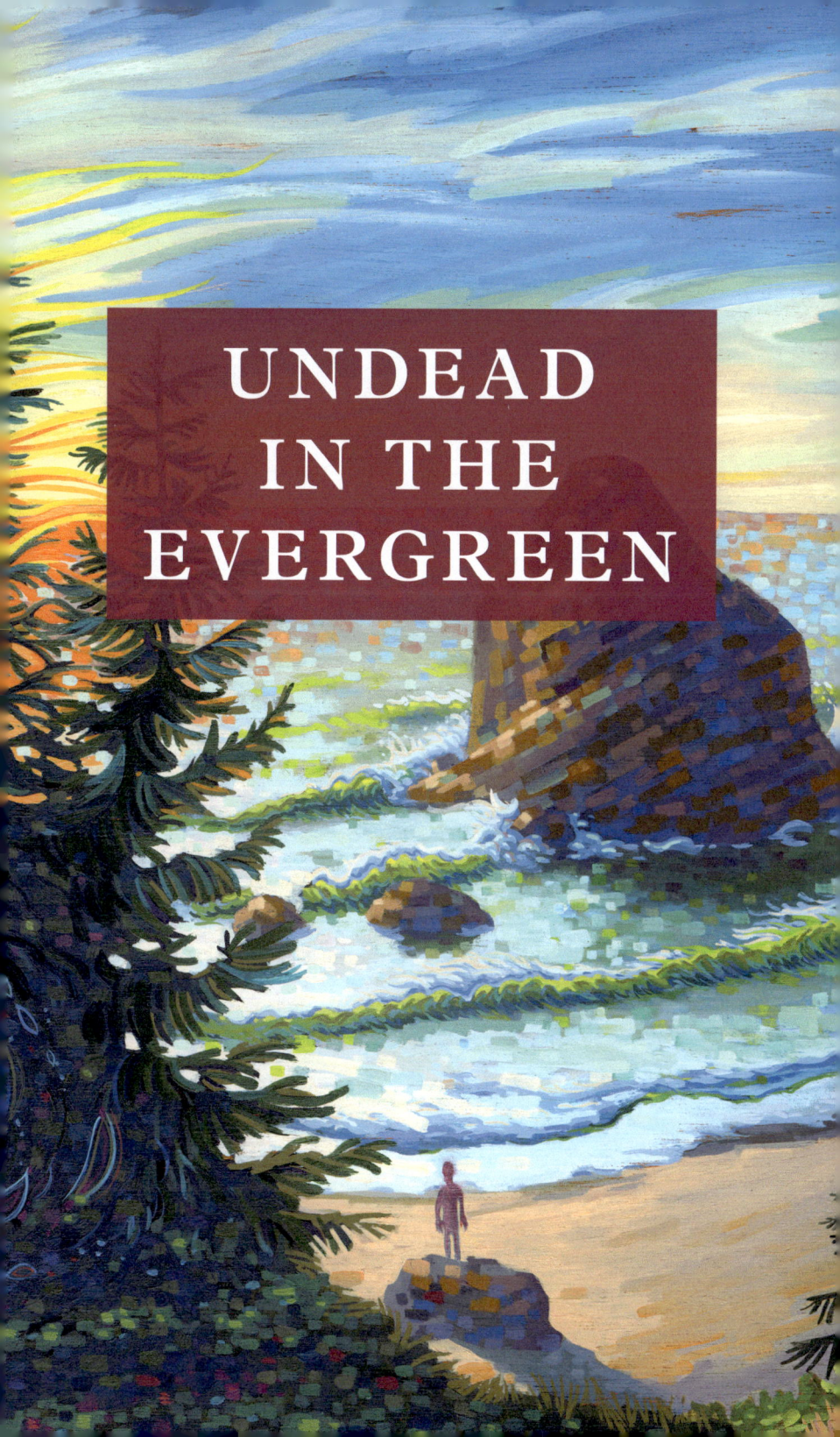

Pope Gregory's calendar—let's study the strangeness of it. Of its static continuum. Its atomized hive mind of time—of everything we assume earthly. Of what you and I have ever known.

Nights with smoked salmon and oatmeal stout and Islay whisky—storm winds whistle on down the stovepipe and winter again is born anew.

Gray daylight—walk in the woods, look around. Ask the dirt: What is a year?

= shallow cycle of Earth 'round Sun. Twelve months/52 weeks/365 solar days/8,760 hours/525,600 minutes/31,536,000 seconds. Ins and outs—highs and lows—fires and snows.

"Calendar": Latin *calendarium*—"interest register," "account book". "December" (Latin *decem*—"ten").

Days 1-10: Twenty-five inches of rain 'pon Purpledeneye Prairie, its clay muds and rocks and vadose zones spilling into my mind maze—my serenity—my mood memory.

December is a memo.

December mnemonia: *A Charlie Brown Christmas*, George C. Scott and his snowy Scrooge London, *Morning of the Earth*, *A Christmas Story*, *It's a Wonderful Life*, *How the Grinch Stole Christmas!*, "The Little Fir Tree", late boozy readings of "The Night Before Christmas", antique balls and bells, treetop angels, "Gnomes", board games, laughs, deaths, scented candles, cats, horses, breweries, bowls of candy, citrus scent of Douglas fir, needlepoint stockings, Enya, family parties, drunken arguments, hangovers, colored lights, advent calendars with chocolate treats, build-ups and let-downs, gold-rimmed plates, guests, champagne toasts and tears in soft glow, Mme Fleur's fancy fare and firm handshakes, neckties, poinsettias, green needles on white carpets, red wine, cozy eves aside purring flames, apple pie and peppermint ice cream, baking cookies with siblings, wreaths on the front door, grandmother's noble fir and fluttering gas fireplace, turkey dinners, mimosa breakfasts, burnt bacon, Rita Ford's Music Boxes over and over on the antique turntable.

Days 11-20: Topaz trinities torch the rivermouth ether—glare, sand, Sun. Gravel bar as eventual ghost. Stroke into the rights as they pitch and teeth through the cold offshores. Dawns of amethyst. Apt for a December dry spell.

Again clouds will soak and gather the world around us.

Home. Shoveling to quell erosion. Newly planted seedlings of pine and incense cedar, coffeeberry, ceanothus. Tallying rainfall and draining bottles of petite sirah.

Day 21: *sol* = Latin for "sun"—*sistere* = "to stand still"—*solstitium* = chrysalis to "solstice" and the astrological winter begins.

Surf is sought. It is bad. Clear sky. The opening of closure. More rain en route.

Days 22-27: mnemonia. The full Cold Moon comes and goes.

I raise and redrop the stylus onto life's spinning disk.

December is a world.

One primordial to the tones and bones beneath House Rock Viewpoint, a Western Gate sort of place due west of my drunken head which rests nightly upon a psychic map.

Kindred land is remembered. 570 miles to my southeast lies Point Conception, aka Humqaq, a burr on California's hip. Was and is the Western Gate per its legends and spirit flight to infinitude, anciently revered in the nearby Chumash villages of 'Upop and Shilimazshtush. For them, Humqaq was a south-west-facing land's-end eye to sacrality, a portal to the hereafter to glowing eternity, a rainbow bridge—not a divide—to Shimilaqsha: realm of the dead.

Remains unknown whether the Chetco and/or tribes of Tututni (Pistol River to Port Orford/Sixes zone) sensed the same from any areal headlands—Point St. George, Chetco Point, Crook Point, Cape Sebastian, Cape Blanco.

I sense they did.

Day 28: Muddy descent. Loud surf. Walk and grok nature's equanimity. Slick greenmossy roots in the thin path north to Whaleshead—a trail trailing tribal tears—they too knew the thunders of a 25-foot swell at 20 seconds. Deep thoracic radiation into the clifftop colonnades wherever the groves dip low enough into bowling lees sheltered from southeast wind which otherwise blow aquatic bass notes back out to the naked west.

Slow-mo swells rib to horizon in the solemn mute-gray of afternoon. Lower feels in elevated substrate: salal, silktassel, coyote bush. Sword fern and huckleberry in situational cusps of sunlight. Look—northforth undulations of the immediate Coast Range—air temp mild per south flow and the scaly salt-sprayed Sitka *(Picea sitchensis)* bark and branches do groan and greech in the widowmaking wind.

A small city in southeast Alaska, Sitka is also a Tlingit tribe. Where is their Western Gate?

Feels sacred to convalesce amongst such soul-shadows: a friend's Sitka guitar soundboard; boyhood model airplanes made of Sitka; an old neighbor's gorgeous home Sitka flooring. My memory bank screams with this most Cascadian of conifer, the first that truly gripped my mind after I zoomed up from SoCal in the mid-1990s.

With pines and firs and other evergreens, Sitkas colonized this primeval shore, sprouting from post-glacial moraines in the Pleistocene aside the evolution of us anatomically modern humans. *Picea sitchensis* is Earth's third-biggest tree (#1 coast redwood, #2 Douglas fir)—shallow root spawl creates rainforest—herein the Spruce Coast—which from the Lost Coast to Tolowa Dee-ni' lies concomitant with California's Redwood Coast—veering and spearing itself deepnorth into the wilds of Kodiak Isle.

Mnemonia: savor its strangeness.

Days 29-31: Journey with Jill to fecund Humbug Mountain around which snakes a robust Brush Creek. To Dragonfly Farm for more seedlings of incense cedar. To little Langlois for "world famous" hot dogs. To Cape Blanco—the Tututni Western Gate?

Like Point Conception, Blanco is a hard biogeographic break—where the north-south reach of certain species start or end—in the California Current Regional Ecosystem. Here we gaze upon the black backlit rocks of Orford Reef and squint west into the soft orange shimmer of memorial light for life that is always swept out toward crystal marine mountains. Unslain spirit worlds of the future, much like the ends of years and resolutions and hopefulness or hopelessness to come within the next 12 flips of futurity— Gregorian calendar.

We flip homebound before dark. New Year's Eve golden hour at Port Orford (pop. 1,200) where two surfers bob off the basalt promontory called Battle Rock. The waves are small and clean but poorly shaped. The site was named for a terrible whites-on-Indians slaughter in 1851 after Capt. William Tichenor of the *Sea Gull* dropped nine men at this scenic south-facing cove to peg a port for the burgeoning gold rush. Hence the Oregon Coast's first white settlement/land grab. Was named for George Walpole, third Earl of Orford (village in southeast England) and pal of George Vancouver, Royal Navy captain who in the 1790s had charted the zone.

Zooming south to Brookings/Chetco my mind charts the heavens of this elysian coast back from the mystifying eve of time itself. Theoretical physics leads me through gravity's journey and the omniscience of these constellations borne through a fireball explosion. The Big Bang 13.8 billion years ago to nonstop Universe expansion via clumping of dark matter and cosmic dark ages to the accretion of gas clouds to the birth of stars (small galaxies) to the merging of those galaxies to the billions upon billions of elliptical and spiral galaxies to all 8.1 billion of us—we being the children of stardust.

December is a door.

And time yawns mnemonic. Darkness to light—birth to death—to the dusk and dawn of every single new year. What is a year? Presence. It's all a Western Gate, indeed a portal to the hereafter. Sacramental time. A springboard. Constellations of memory, of serendipity. Calendars will always flip themselves.

Over Point St. George

Cape Blanco

House Rock

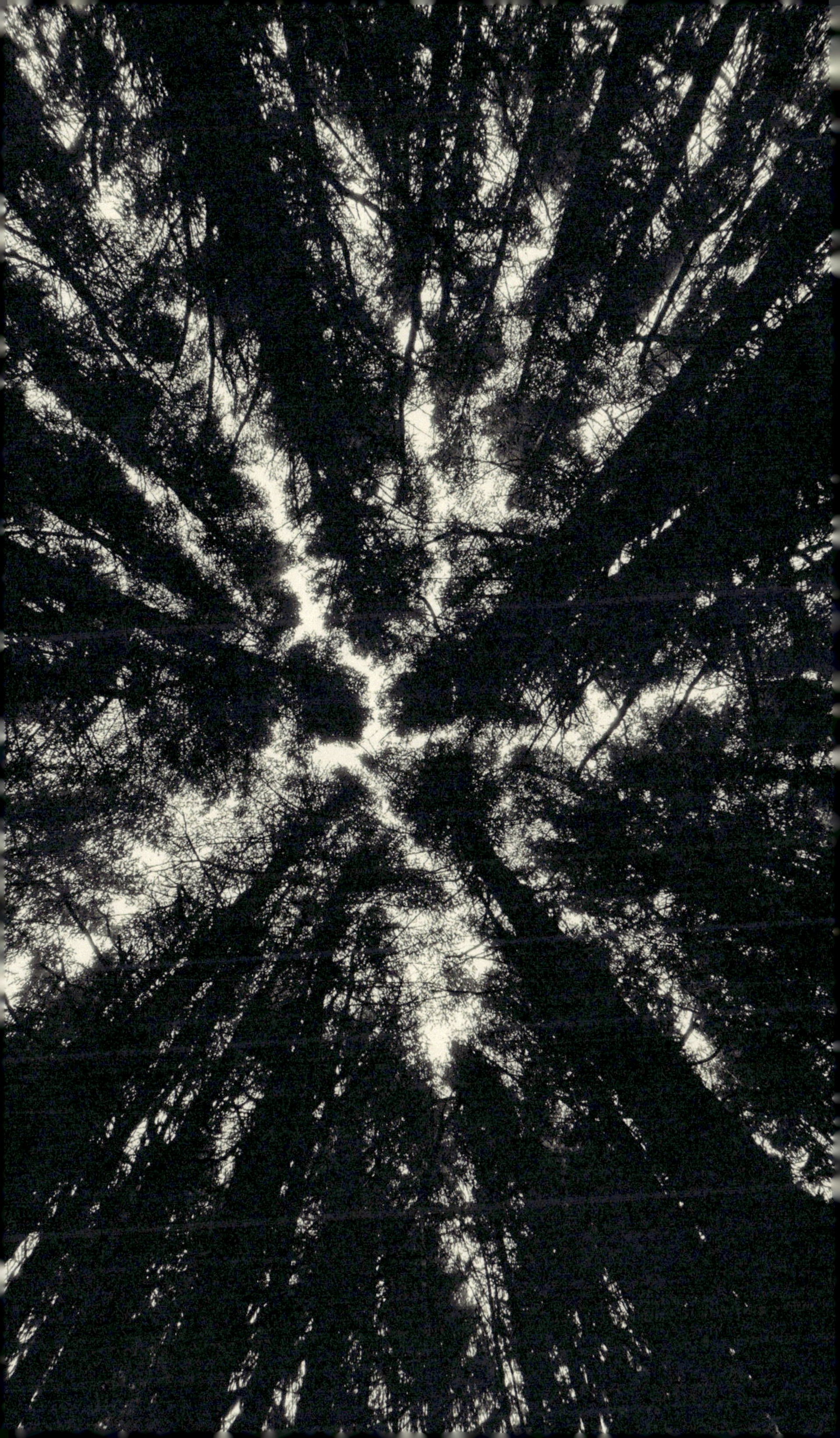

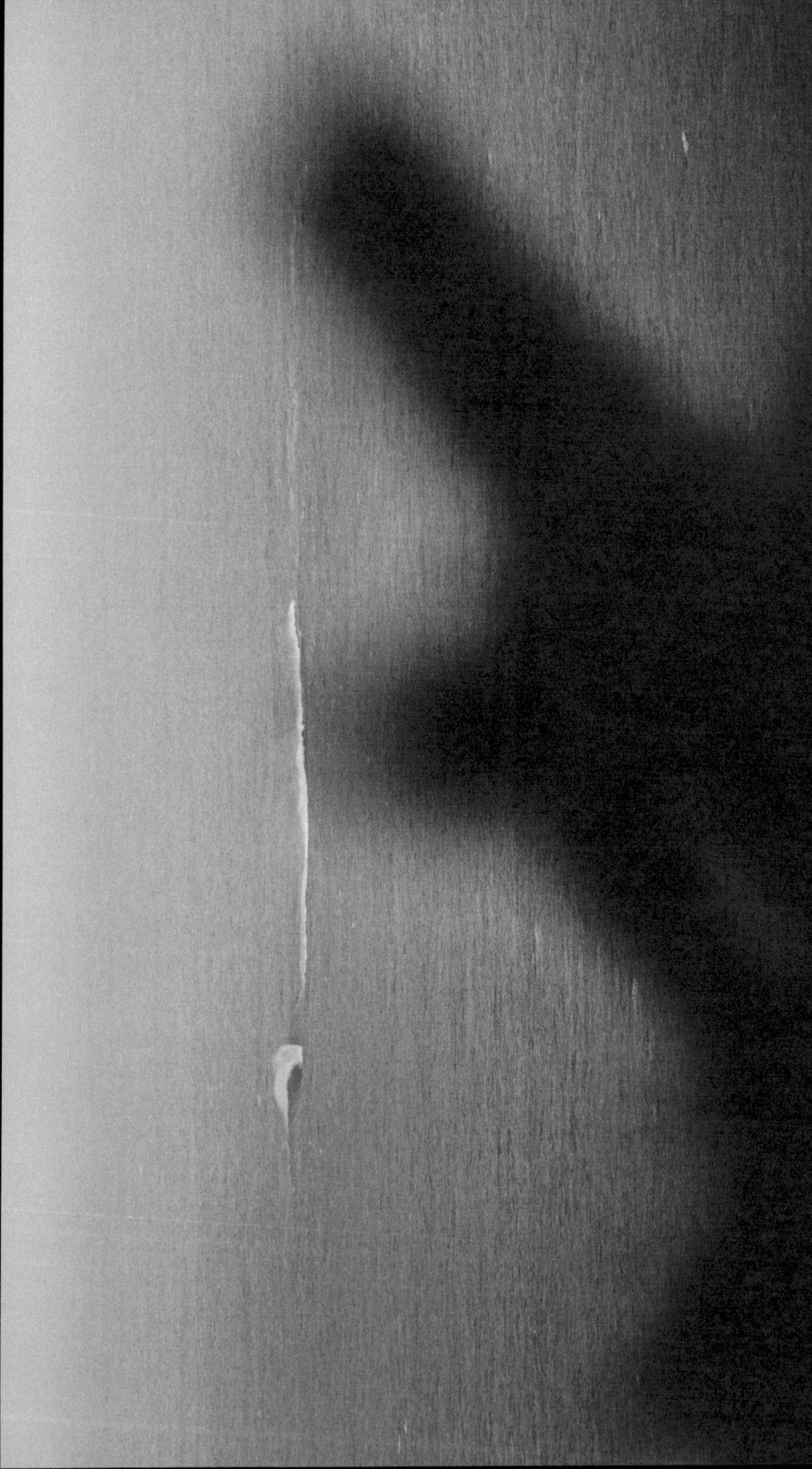

Luke Mathison, SUP on Vulcan Lake.
photo: Dillon Jenkins

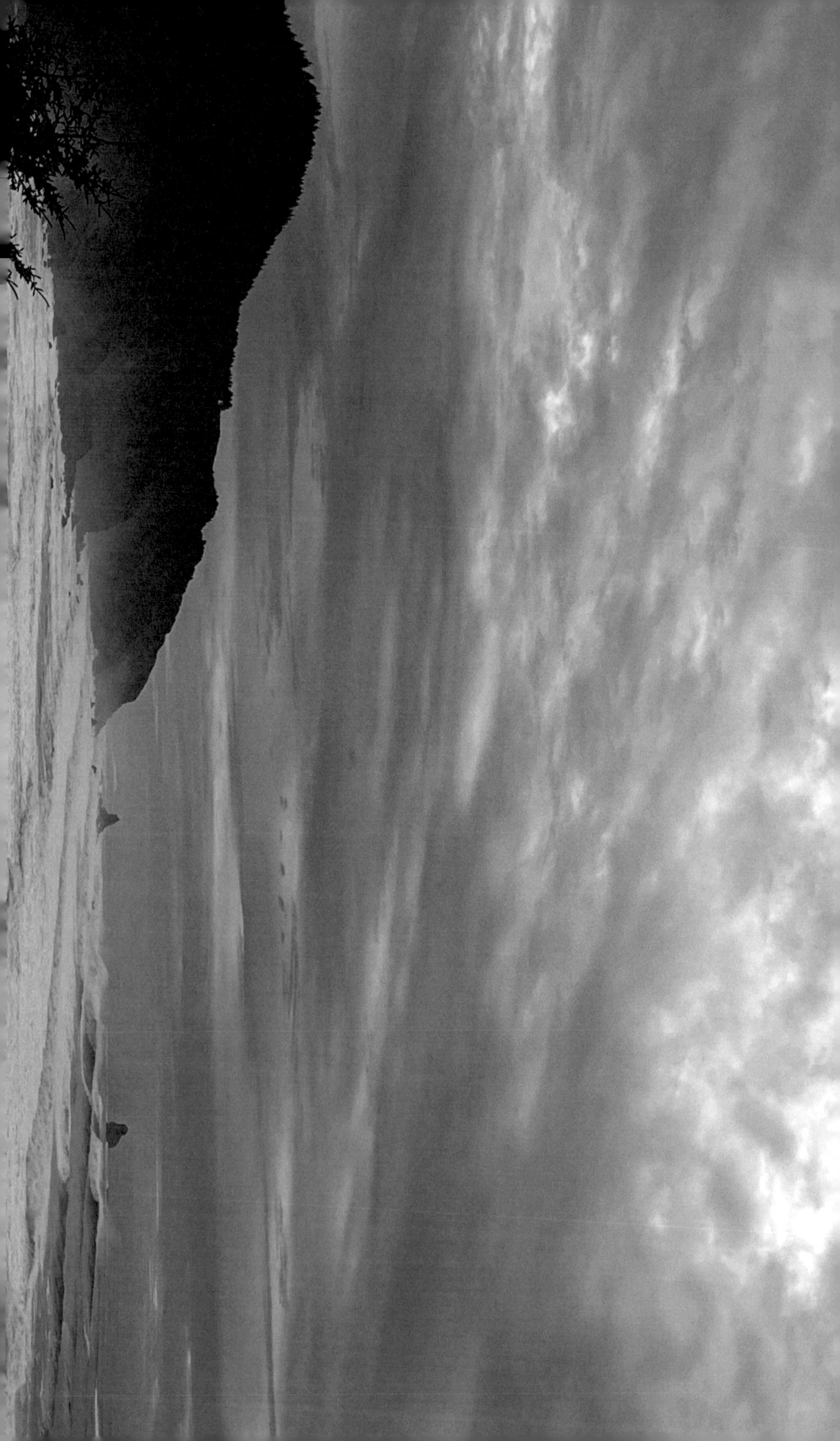

Sitka spruce

George Law Curry
Courtesy Oregon Hist. Soc. Research Lib., 5219

ABOUT CURRY COUNTY

*courtesy of the Curry Historical Society and
the Oregon Historical Society*

Curry County is situated along the Pacific Coast in the southwestern corner of Oregon. It is bounded on the south by California's Del Norte County, on the west by the Pacific Ocean, on the north by Coos County, and on the east by Josephine County. Created on Dec. 18, 1855, the county originally contained about 1,500 square miles. However, boundary adjustments with Coos County in 1872 and 1951 and with Josephine County in 1880 and 1927 would increase the area to 1,648 square miles.

Initially it was proposed that the new county be named after Capt. William Tichenor, council member from Port Orford. However, he declined because his constituents wanted to honor the territorial governor, George Law Curry (1820-1878).

Curry's primary goal had been the settlement of southwestern and eastern Oregon in the face of Indian resistance. When white incursions into the area led to conflict, Curry repeatedly demanded federal troops and funding for local militias. Criticism of his policies in eastern newspapers inspired him to condemn the "newspaper editors of the refined east, where the chiefest danger to life arises from *voluptuous living, who know the Indian character only through poetry and romance" and who had no conception of the dangers settlers faced. He added: "It is painful to conclude that the success of the whites, in repelling the attacks of the ruthless invader, was less gratifying to such mental organizations than would have been the depopulation of both territories by Indian conquest."*

Curry earned support through his careful respect for the elected legislature and its prerogatives. He encouraged the efforts to win statehood for Oregon and, when it was achieved, was succeeded by newly elected governor John Whiteaker. After Curry narrowly missed being elected a U.S. senator in 1860, he returned to the newspaper business as editor of the Portland Advertiser, *one of several Oregon newspapers suppressed by the federal government for suspected opposition to the Civil War.*

Upon creation of Curry County, the Territorial Legislature fixed the county seat temporarily at Port Orford until the citizens of the county could determine a permanent site. In 1859, following an informal vote of county citizens during the general election, Ellensburg was designated the county seat. In 1891 Ellensburg was renamed Gold Beach because of the gold and other minerals found in the sands in this area and to eliminate confusion with the city of Ellensburg located in the state of Washington.

The first courthouse was in Judge Fred Smith's home in Port Orford. Apparently the town's inability to finance the construction of a proper courthouse was a factor in the vote that favored the move to Gold Beach. The first courthouse in Gold Beach was replaced in 1912. The current courthouse was constructed in 1958.

The government of Curry County consisted originally of a probate judge, a three-member board of commissioners, sheriff, auditor, treasurer, and coroner. The county judge's position was replaced by a board of commissioners in 1969. Port districts were established at Port Orford in 1919, Gold Beach in 1955, and Brookings-Harbor in 1956.

The first county census in 1860 showed a human population of 393; the 2024 population is approximately 23,000.

Approximately two-thirds of Curry County are national forests and grasslands. The county is home to five National Wild and Scenic Rivers: Elk, Rogue, Illinois, Chetco, and North Fork Smith—all renowned for their clear water, salmon runs, and recreation opportunities. The county is also home to four wilderness areas: Kalmiopsis, Wild Rogue, Grassy Knob, and Copper Salmon. The marine-influenced climate is characterized by mild year-round temperatures, dry summers, and wet winters. In some spots, annual rainfall can exceed 200 inches.

In 1852 explorers discovered gold and other precious metals in the rivers and along the beaches of this area. Initially settlement in the county was concentrated along the coast and depended primarily on water transportation. The slow development of inland transportation routes kept the county relatively isolated well into the 20th century. While there is still some mining of cobalt, nickel, and chromium in the Gasquet Mountain area, the economy has reoriented to agriculture and timber. The county has excellent grazing areas for raising cattle and sheep. It also produces berries, horticultural nursery stock, and most of the Easter lilies raised in the United States. Vacation and recreational possibilities in the county draw tourists to the area and provide economic diversity.

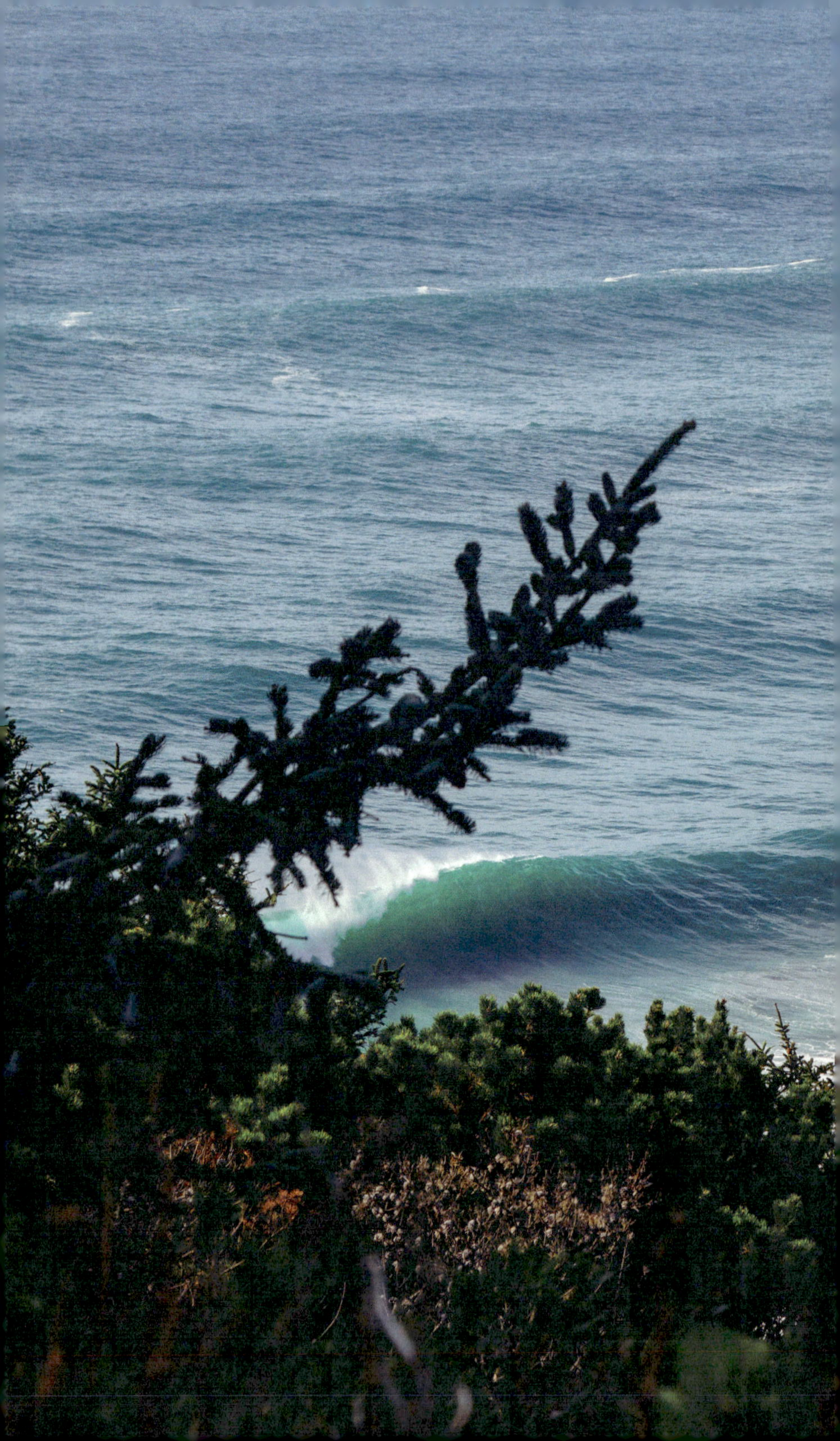

JILL ELLIOTT

Passionate about surfing and travel, MICHAEL H. KEW first tapped his writerly destiny as a Californian boy in the mid-1980s. His work has since been featured Earthwide in magazines, newspapers, films, websites, advertisements, and books. He lives at Purplēdeneye in the green mountains of Curry County.

Made in the USA
Columbia, SC
16 December 2024

329a8b7c-7a0f-4c1d-a73d-d39598e7bf41R01